Writing up your University Assignments and Research Projects

A practical handbook

Writing up your University Assignments and Research Projects

A practical handbook

Neil Murray and Geraldine Hughes

 Open University Press

Open University Press
McGraw-Hill Education
McGraw-Hill House
Shoppenhangers Road
Maidenhead
Berkshire
England
SL6 2QL

email: enquiries@openup.co.uk
world wide web: www.openup.co.uk

and Two Penn Plaza, New York, NY 10121-2289, USA

First published 2008

A catalogue record of this book is available from the British Library

ISBN-13: 978–0335–22717–4 (pb)   978–0335–22718–1 (hb)
ISBN-10: 0–335–22717–1 (pb)   0–335–22718–x (hb)

Library of Congress Cataloguing-in-Publication Data
CIP data applied for

Typeset by RefineCatch Limited, Bungay, Suffolk
Printed in Great Britain by Bell and Bain Ltd, Glasgow

Fictious names of companies, products, people, characters and/or
data that may be used herein (in case studies or in examples) are not
intended to represent any real individual, company, product or event.

The *McGraw·Hill* Companies

Contents

Acknowledgements

This book is the result of contributions from numerous people and institutions, all of whom deserve our sincerest thanks. First, the staff and students of the English Language Centre and the Geography and War Studies departments at King's College London, who both inspired it and offered unerring support during its development. Particular thanks go to Tony Thorne, Robert Hydon and Helen Fisher, and to Faye and Alexander Murray, two younger members of our 'support team' whose IT expertise both helped us immensely and filled us with considerable humility! To Averil Coxhead we extend our appreciation for permission to include the Academic Word List featured in the book's Appendix. We are also extremely grateful to Robert Greenhill and Anne Furlong for their generosity in extending us permission to use extracts of their PhD theses for illustrative purposes, and to King's College London for permission to draw on the theses of James Griffiths and Pamela Vass for examples of good practice. Although we were unable to contact Drs Griffiths and Vass despite extensive efforts, we hope they feel, like us, that their 'contributions' are a valuable addition to the book.

Last, but by no means least, we owe a great debt of thanks to Melanie Havelock, Commissioning Editor at McGraw-Hill, for her confidence in and support of the project from the outset. Her efficiency and sensitivity have smoothed the passage of the book from a fairly ragged first draft to what we hope is a rather more polished final product, and made the whole process nothing but a positive experience. We are similarly grateful to the reviewers of the manuscript and to all staff at McGraw-Hill involved in the book's production, marketing and sales, and in particular Lin Gillan, Product Manager for the Study Skills list.

Foreword

Who is the book for?

Whether you are an undergraduate or postgraduate student, a native speaker or a non-native speaker, fresh out of high school or a mature student returning after years away from academic life, the prospect of writing college or university assignments and/or writing up a research project can be a daunting one which, understandably, often causes anxiety and prompts many questions. Faced with writing projects that can range from 2000 to 100,000 words, many students quickly find themselves struggling to cope and in need of clear, straightforward guidance. Quite naturally, they often turn first to their lecturers, tutors or supervisors, only to find that much as they might wish to help, their own ever-increasing workload – and sometimes lack of linguistic expertise – often prevents them from being able to offer the level of support necessary and, as a result, students can be left fending for themselves and feeling uncertain, isolated and helpless. In the worst cases, this can lead to intense frustration, panic and, ultimately, even despair and failure. Where students who face difficulties do manage to submit work, lecturers and supervisors can be left struggling to understand it. In-house English language and study skills support classes are often over-subscribed and tend to focus primarily (and often inadequately) on non-native speakers, while private institutions tend to offer only general writing courses and can be costly.

This guide is our attempt to address this problem by providing a carefully structured and comprehensive programme of self-study that is accessible to both native and non-native speakers of English and which responds to the needs of undergraduate as well as postgraduate students. It is designed to develop not only your understanding of the mechanics of writing, but also your ability to be critical about your own writing through systematically raising your awareness of the many different facets of the writing process, from grammatical structure, punctuation and vocabulary, to an understanding and appreciation of the broader principles of good writing – coherence and good argument structure, an awareness of style and register, and formatting conventions, to name just a few. Most importantly, it strives to help you develop a sense of autonomy, control and self-confidence.

How is the book organized?

The book is divided into 3 main parts as follows:

Part 1 presents the fundamentals of good academic writing, including a detailed description of the various functions writing performs and the words and phrases associated with them, as well as an explanation of the building blocks of academic writing and guidance on how to structure your writing correctly and effectively. In addition, it focuses on more advanced issues relating to writing style, referencing and layout.

Part 2 presents an initial introduction to the research process and the writing-up of research, followed by an analysis and explanation of the various parts or stages of a research report, from the title page to the bibliography and appendices. In addition, it offers a chapter on getting your work published, along with suggestions for doing so.

Part 3 contains a 'Toolkit' consisting of a simple guide to punctuation use, a glossary of key terms, Coxhead's Academic Word List, a list of prefixes and suffixes with their meanings, and an Appendix with style guide resources/links for referencing, as well as sample materials.

Other key features of the book include:

- accessible explanations;
- strategies and tips for more efficient and effective writing;
- multiple examples, many of which are authentic;
- tasks designed to test your understanding of what you have read and provide you with opportunities to practise what you have learnt.

How to use the book

We have tried to structure the book incrementally such that each part builds upon what has gone before. Nevertheless, each part essentially works also as a stand-alone section or 'unit' and as such you can 'dip into' the book at any point in order to gain clarification on a particular aspect of writing. We should emphasize, though, that however you choose to use the book, it is important that you read all the *Writing Tips* and *Notes* (indicated by the pen and notepad icons respectively) and attempt as many of the *Tasks* as possible. Both are a crucial part of the learning process adopted in the book. The Writing Tips contain important information, and the tasks give you an opportunity to test your understanding. Suggested answers to the tasks can be found at the end of each of the sections in which tasks have been set. In the book's Appendix, we have included Coxhead's *Academic Word List*, a list of those words most frequently used in academic discourse, along with an explanation of how it may assist you in your writing.

A final word

Finally, a word of caution: although there are rules and conventions that guide us in our writing, these are rarely as absolute as textbooks would have us believe; consequently, you will quite frequently come across instances where they appear to be flouted. Who can flout the rules and when is a complex issue beyond the remit of this guide. Suffice it to say that it is only via exposure through reading and by a process of trial and error that you will acquire an understanding of the many exceptions to rules and the often very subtle circumstances in which they occur.

You should also remember that there can be some variation between academic disciplines in the conventions and expectations that apply to the writing of assignments, dissertations and theses, and it is therefore important to consult carefully with your colleagues, tutors, supervisors and university information services in order to ensure that you are fully aware of the conventions that apply specifically to your own field of study.

We hope very much that you find this guide helpful and wish you luck with your writing projects.

Neil Murray (University of South Australia)
Geraldine Hughes (King's College London)

A guide to the book's icons: what do they mean?

We have suggested in the Foreword that you read all of the Writing Tips and Notes that appear throughout the book; these can be identified via the icons that accompany them. We would like to take a moment to clarify exactly what these icons mean and what kind of information they signal.

 Writing Tips

Where you see this icon, you will find a short piece of advice about how you can improve your writing. Often the information emphasizes or highlights a particular point, or provides 'additional' information not always featured in more general discussions of academic writing. It includes strategies for writing more effectively and efficiently, and alerts to help you avoid common pitfalls. These 'Writing Tips', then, focus specifically on the actual mechanics of writing and are therefore instructional or procedural in nature; they tell you *how* to do things, and our purpose in including them is to pass on to you 'tips' that we – and others – have picked up over years of writing in an academic context and of marking students' work.

 Notes

Unlike the Writing Tips, Notes do not focus specifically on the mechanics of writing and are not instructional or procedural in nature. Instead, where you see these icons, you will find observations about, or brief insights into, different aspects of the processes of writing up assignments and research projects, notes of caution, reminders, and ideas to help you think about and assess your writing.

 Task Keys

These icons signal answer keys to the tasks set in the book. You will find these icons appearing within a shaded box at the end of sections in which tasks have been set. Note that solutions to tasks will not be given in cases where you are required to do your own research (for example, analysing a piece of writing of your own choice with a view to identifying a particular feature).

Part 1

THE FUNDAMENTALS OF ACADEMIC WRITING

1

What are the key functions in academic writing?

1.1 Introduction • 1.2 Defining terms and ideas (see also Section 4.6) • 1.3 Describing • 1.4 Comparing and contrasting • 1.5 Classifying • 1.6 Explaining causes and effects • 1.7 Developing an argument

1.1 Introduction

If you read any piece of academic writing, whether it is an essay, a journal article, a dissertation, a thesis or a book, you will find that it contains a number of clearly distinguishable 'types' of writing within it. These types reflect the objectives – or *functions* – you are trying to achieve at different stages of your work, and they include *definition, description, classification, cause–effect, comparison and contrast*, and *argumentation*. Particularly in longer pieces of writing, such as a research report, most of these functions will feature at some point and your report will therefore be made up of a complex network of these types used in combination. Furthermore, one function may form an integral part of another function; for example, you may use *classification* or *comparison and contrast* as part of a *description*.

Being able to think about our writing explicitly in terms of the different functions it is performing at different stages can help us in two ways. First, it can help us categorize or 'label' different sections of our writing and in doing so serves as an organizational framework according to which we can place those sections in the most logical, readable order. For example, a definition tends to precede a description: you will most likely want to define what 'hybrid automotive technology' is *before* you explain its purpose and how it works. Second, having established the particular function with which you are working at any particular time, this knowledge can serve as a cue for the introduction of the appropriate words and phrases commonly used to help express that function.

What follows is an explanation of the functions mentioned earlier, together with some examples of the kind of language typically associated with each. It is a good idea to try and familiarize yourself with as many of these words and phrases as possible so that you can deploy them quickly and easily during the course of your writing.

1.2 Defining terms and ideas (see also Section 4.6)

In academic writing it is necessary to define specialized, controversial or ambiguous terminology, and to use it consistently in your writing. This is important because the same term may take on different meanings depending on the context in which it is used. Furthermore, there can be slight and often subtle variations in the way different writers use the same term and what they mean by it. You should therefore ensure that you make absolutely clear the meanings you are assigning to key terms used in your writing, particularly if you are using them in a way that differs from the generally accepted definition. Very occasionally, the definition of terminology can lie at the heart of an essay or research project the very purpose of which may be to provide clarification of a particular term. This can and should be made evident early on in your work, in the Abstract (in the case of a research report) and/or the Introduction (see Section 6).

Another reason why the precise definition of key terms is so important is that those terms will form an integral part of the assumptions, claims and lines of argument underlying your thesis statement – your main claim or line of argument (see Section 2.2). As such they indirectly play a significant part in persuading the reader of the validity of your ideas.

At a more practical level, defining terms can serve three other purposes. First, where there is a general consensus on their meaning and little or no room for the kind of variation mentioned earlier, it can be used to demonstrate your understanding of the concepts to which they refer. Second, it can be a useful strategy for getting started – something many writers often find difficult. In this way, definitions often serve as 'stepping-off' points; a way of launching into your discussion. And, where appropriate, it may be helpful to quote an authority or two in the field when providing your definition. Finally, a definition can help give structure to a piece of writing. Look at the following example:

The Romance languages might perhaps be defined collectively as a linguistic consequence of the Roman Empire. In furtherance of our purpose, which is to explore in some detail the substance of this definition, it seems appropriate to determine, as a preliminary step, with what languages we shall be concerned and why they are called 'Romance'.

(Elcock, 1960: 17)

A definition can be short (one or two sentences) or long (several paragraphs or even a complete chapter) depending on the complexity of the term(s) you are attempting to explain, the degree of variation with which it has been used in the literature, and whether clarification of the term is a major goal of your study.

 When defining a term, a useful strategy is to fit the term you are describing into a category followed by its distinguishing characteristics.

Here are some examples of fairly short, simple definitions:

Example: A volcanian type of <u>volcanic eruption</u> (*category*) is characterized by violent gas explosions which cause plugs of sticky or cooled lava to be ejected (*distinguishing characteristics*).

Example: Plate tectonics involves theories (*category*) which describe and explain the distribution of volcanoes, earthquakes, foldouts and continental drift (*distinguishing characteristics*).

Example: Stagflation describes a situation (*category*) where high inflation and high unemployment exist at a time of poor economic growth (*distinguishing characteristics*).

TASK 1

Complete the chart below. Then, write a one-sentence definition of each term listed in the left column. The first one has been done for you as an example:

TERM	CATEGORY	CHARACTERISTICS
1. Manufacturing industries	*secondary sector*	*make finished products*
2. Service industries		
3. Impressionism		

(continued overleaf)

TERM	CATEGORY	CHARACTERISTICS
4. International aid		
5. Development gap		
6. Biodiversity		
7. Bilateral agreement		
8. Non-renewable resources		
9. Corporate culture		
10. Management by objectives		
11. Gross Domestic Product (GDP)		
12. Inward investment		

1. *Manufacturing industries are secondary sector industries which process or assemble components to make finished products.*

A more detailed definition will often include the origin of the term, a brief history of its development, a description of how it functions, and possibly an explanation of its uses.

 A definition uses description and often elements of comparison and contrast and classification (discussed later in this section).

Look at the following example in which an abstract concept, 'imagination', is defined. Notice how the writer compares and contrasts human imagination with that of animals in order to narrow down and make clearer the meaning of the term as well as give a more refined definition of human imagination in particular.

Example

> We all dream. That is imagination at work. To imagine means simply to make an image – a picture – in our minds. Human beings are not the only creatures who have imagination. Even animals dream. Cats' ears and tails may twitch as they sleep and sleeping dogs may whine and growl and paw the air as if they were having a fight. Even when awake, animals 'see' things . . . Clearly, however, there is a profound difference between human and animal imagination. Humans are the only creatures who can tell one another about imagination in stories or pictures. The urge to make art is unique to us.
>
> (Jansen, 1995: 16)

In the next example, in order to provide a more precise definition of the term 'harmonisation', the writer contrasts it with the concept of 'mutual recognition':

> Harmonisation of regulation can be defined as the development of common regulatory principles, laws and rules across jurisdictions. Harmonisation contrasts with mutual recognition. In the latter, practices and principles recognised within one jurisdiction are recognised within others. For example, under mutual recognition, a French insurance company could trade in the UK, regulated by the French authorities, even though French regulation might be different from UK regulation. The UK authorities 'recognise' French regulation and, in turn, the French authorities 'recognise' UK regulation.
>
> (Booth and Currie, 2003: 123)

1.2.1 Words and phrases associated with definition

The following expressions are frequently used to introduce definitions and clarify meaning. The list is not comprehensive and there are many other often more complex ways of performing this function in writing:

By X is meant . . .
I am taking X to mean . . .
. . ., namely, . . .
In the present study, X refers to . . .
The term as used here refers not to . but instead/rather to . . .
This term refers to . . .
Although there have been various interpretations of X, I am using it to mean . . .
*There has been a good deal of variation in the literature in the way in which the
    term X has been used. In this study I am taking it to mean (specifically) . . .*
*X, notably relating to . . . as opposed to Y, is used in this report/work/thesis to refer
    to . . .*
In other words,
In this respect, . . .
In this sense, . . .

TASK 2

a) Use the information on photosynthesis and respiration given below to complete the gap-fill exercise that follows it. You may use more than one word in each space. The terms 'photosynthesis' and 'respiration' are defined by comparing and contrasting them with each other.

PHOTOSYNTHESIS	RESPIRATION
1. Combines carbon dioxide and water	1. Uses oxygen and glucose
2. Produces glucose and oxygen	2. Produces carbon dioxide and water
3. Can only occur in light	3. Can occur in both light and darkness
4. Occurs only in cells containing chlorophyll	4. Occurs in all living cells
5. Requires energy (in the form of light)	5. Releases energy

Photosynthesis can be .... as the process whereby plants combine .... from the air with .... absorbed .... their roots. The .... of photosynthesis are glucose and ...., with the latter being released as a by-product. Respiration is the reverse process. It requires both .... and glucose and releases ...., producing both carbon dioxide and .... as by-products. Unlike photosynthesis, this process can occur in both .... and ...., as the process does not require light energy. Whereas .... can only occur in cells containing chlorophyll, respiration will occur in all ....

---

b) Write an extended definition of a term, explaining how it will be used within the context of your research report, and making clear your own particular interpretation of the term.

 TASK KEY

TASK 1   (Possible answers)

1. Manufacturing industries are secondary-sector industries which process or assemble components to make finished products.
2. Service industries are tertiary-sector industries that provide a facility or service rather than manufactured goods.
3. Impressionism is a nineteenth century movement in painting, the characteristics of which are visible brush strokes and an emphasis upon the changing qualities of light.
4. International aid is the provision of expertise, manufactured goods, food or money by developed nations to those in the developing world.
5. The development gap is the difference in economic activity and wealth which exists between developed and developing countries.
6. Biodiversity is a term used to refer to the number and variety of different species of plant and animal life within one particular region or the earth as a whole.
7. A bilateral agreement is an agreement created between two states or institutions.

8. Non-renewable resources are natural resources, such as minerals and fossil fuels, which are in limited supply.
9. Corporate culture is the term given to the values, beliefs and norms that are shared by those who work in a particular organization.
10. Management by objectives (MBO) is a management theory whereby managers set goals and communicate them to their subordinates.
11. Gross Domestic Product is a term used in economics to refer to the total value of goods and services produced by a country over a one-year period.
12. Inward investment refers to the flow of funds into a country from overseas for the purpose of setting up business operations.

TASK 2a

Photosynthesis can be <u>defined</u> as the process whereby plants combine <u>carbon dioxide</u> from the air with <u>water</u> absorbed <u>through/by</u> their roots. The <u>products</u> of photosynthesis are glucose and <u>oxygen</u>, with the latter being released as a by-product. Respiration is the reverse process. It requires both <u>oxygen</u> and glucose and releases <u>energy</u>, producing both carbon dioxide and <u>water</u> as by-products. Unlike photosynthesis, this process can occur in both <u>light</u> and <u>darkness</u>, as the process does not require light energy. Whereas <u>photosynthesis</u> can only occur in cells containing chlorophyll, respiration will occur in all <u>living cells</u>.

1.3 Describing

1.3.1 Describing processes

Description can take many forms in academic writing. In scientific and technical writing it usually involves explaining how to do or make something: for example, how to conduct an experiment, how to construct a dam, how to operate a machine or how to carry out a manufacturing process. And in a research report, of course, it will be used to describe the methodology employed in the course of your research (see Section 6.8). This type of description is referred to as 'process' description because it describes a series of steps that need to be carried out in a particular order. Sequence linking words and phrases are therefore used to connect each step in the process:

First(ly), . . .	*Second(ly), . . .*	*Third(ly), . . .*	*Next, . . .*
Then, . . .	*After this, . . .*	*Finally/Lastly, . . .*	*Prior to . . .*
Following . . .	*While . . .*	*Simultaneously . . .*	*Before . . .*

 'At last' *means 'eventually' and therefore cannot be used to indicate the final stage of a process.* 'Lastly', *however, can be used as an alternative.*

In process description, the language forms used by the writer will differ in the following two situations:

1. If the description is being provided in order to enable the reader to carry out the process themselves, the imperative form is used ('First, remove . . .; next, insert . . .; finally, unscrew . . .' etc.). In other words, instructions will be given in the form of orders – a form of description typically found in manuals for household appliances and scientific writing.

Example

First, remove the terminal cover and feed the cable through the cable gland. Next, tighten the cable gland to ensure a waterproof seal and secure the cable under the cable clamp. Connect the earth wire to the connector marked 'O', the red phase conductor to the connector marked 'L', and the black neutral conductor to the connector marked 'N'. Finally, check that all connections are correct and refit the terminal cover.

---

2. If the description is merely informative and designed to help the reader understand how a particular operation is performed rather than to enable them to perform it themselves, the passive voice is normally used (*is removed, are inserted, is attached* etc.). This type of description implies that somebody or something other than the reader performs the actions that make up the process described.

Example

One source of sugar for sugar companies such as Tate & Lyle is sugar cane. This has to undergo two processes before it is suitable for human consumption. First, the sugar cane crop is harvested and the cane is extracted in sugar mills. This process is carried out by cutting the cane into small pieces and crushing it between heavy rollers; the shredded cane is then sprayed with hot water to leach out the sugar, which at this stage is a brown juice. To clean the juice, lime is added and it is then filtered to remove any fibre particles and impurities. After this, the juice is boiled under vacuum to produce a thick syrup. The syrup, which is known as molasses, is then separated from the sugar crystals which have formed – these crystals are the raw sugar that is exported for refining. Upon arrival at the sugar refinery, this second stage in sugar production is a crystallisation process whereby several grades of sugar are produced with different crystal sizes. The syrups which remain once the pure sugar has crystallised are used to produce syrup, treacle and soft brown sugar.

TASK 1

Using the information below, describe the sequence of events involved in making a film. Use complete sentences, employ appropriate linking words and phrases between your sentences, and divide your description into paragraphs as indicated. Feel free to change the order of the information and the wording within each paragraph where appropriate.

Paragraph 1

Six main steps:

- finding a property;
- writing a script;
- casting;
- filming;
- editing;
- composing music.

Paragraph 2

Finding a property:

- a 'property' is the story on which the film is to be based;
- property may be original or an adaptation.

Paragraph 3

Writing the script:

- preparing a script is time consuming and lengthy;
- script can be written by original writer or director;
- script writer, producer and director usually work closely together.

Paragraph 4

Casting:

- choose actors and actresses to star in the film;
- either use big international stars or more obscure actors and actresses who have yet to make a name for themselves in the industry.

Paragraph 5

Filming:

- normally takes six to eight months;
- is typically non-chronological;

- takes place on soundstages and on location;
- filming on location is usually extremely expensive.

Paragraph 6

Editing:

- editing is a long and complicated process;
- editor to ensure: the best takes are selected, length of scenes is appropriate, overall pace of film is correct.

Paragraph 7

Composing music:

- a composer is usually called in after editing process is complete;
- composing is difficult as the composer must watch the film and compose music simultaneously;
- soundtrack must be approved by producer and director.

1.3.2 Describing component parts

In addition to describing a process, description can sometimes involve explaining the different elements of which something is composed – for example, the various elements that make up a piece of machinery.

Example

A computer's internal components work together to execute an instruction. A processor contains a clock, an instruction control unit, an arithmetic and logic unit, and several registers, including an instruction counter, an instruction register, and a work register called the accumulator. The computer's other major component, main memory, holds program instructions and data values.

The process starts when the clock generates a pulse of current, which activates the instruction control unit. Its job is to decide what the machine will do next. The computer is controlled by program instructions, and these are stored in main memory. The address of the next instruction to be executed is found in the instruction counter. The instruction control unit checks the instruction counter, finds the address, and fetches the next instruction, placing it in the instruction register. Fetching an instruction from memory takes time, giving the instruction control unit an opportunity to increment the instruction counter to point to the next instruction.

At a precise interval, the clock generates another pulse of current. This one activates the arithmetic and logic unit, which executes the instruction stored in the instruction register.

Following execution of the instruction, a data value is copied from main memory to the accumulator register. Once again, the clock ticks. Thus, it is back to the instruction control unit, where the next machine cycle begins.

(Adapted from Davis 1986)

In this example, the first paragraph describes the internal components of a computer while subsequent paragraphs explain how each component is involved in carrying out an instruction.

 Whereas a description may not always describe a process, a process will always involve description.

TASK 2

Write a description of how a hairdryer works using the information below. Use complete sentences, employ appropriate linking words and phrases between your sentences and divide your description into paragraphs as indicated.

Paragraph 1
Components of a hairdryer:

- heating coil;
- simple motor-driven fan;
- barrel.

Paragraph 2
In conventional hairdryer:

- electrical energy is transformed into convective heat;
- when switched on, current flows through circuit in hairdryer;
- circuit directs power to coiled wire of heating element;
- heating element becomes hot;
- current also makes small electric motor spin;
- electric motor turns the fan.

Paragraph 3
To heat the air:

- an airflow is generated by the fan;
- airflow is directed down the barrel, over and through the heating element;
- air is warmed by the coil via forced convection;
- hot air streams out the end of the barrel.

1.3.3 Describing a sequence of events

Another form of description commonly used in academic writing is chronological description. As the term suggests, this is a description of time sequence – of the order in which events unfold in time. As such it involves words and phrases such as:

before	*subsequently*	*previously*	*at the same time*
after	*prior to*	*later (than)*	*earlier (than)*
next	*simultaneously*	*followed (by)*	*preceded*
in parallel	*X preceded Y*	*X succeeded Y*	*concurrently*
respectively	*later on*		

These words and phrases 'fix' time sequence by indicating when events occurred in relation to each other. Chronological description also includes the description of time frames or time periods, along with associated vocabulary such as:

from . . . to
by . . .
until . . .
during . . .
when . . .
by the time . . .
between . . . and . . .
in (month/year/period) . . . (period: e.g. *in June; in the 1900s; in the Triassic Period; in Shakespeare's time*)
at (precise time of day, e.g. *at 10 o'clock; at midday*)
on (day/date) . . . (date can be either day and month, or day, month and year – e.g. *on 17 October; on 11 March 1988*)
from (year/period/date) *to* (year/period/date) – e.g. *From the Victorian era to the Edwardian era . . .*

Example

When Edward VI came to the throne in 1901 England was a deeply class-ridden society and for each class of people there were very different sorts of housing. During the nineteenth century, the wealthy, upper landed classes tried out a number of different styles in order to follow the changing fashions for the design and decoration of houses during this period. Such people held the firm belief that money invested in land was safe. Then in the 1880s came an influx of cheap corn from America. The result was a drop in demand for English corn and twenty years' depression in English farming. This spelt catastrophe for upper-class families dependent on land and they were forced to find other ways of making money, such as selling off parts of their property and investing in shares.

During this period, the very poor were also affected by the depression. Farm labourers were forced to migrate to the towns in search of work, where they lived in cramped, squalid conditions. This meant that the population of Greater London grew from 3,900,000 in 1871 to 7,300,000 in 1911. To relieve this situation, the 1890s and 1900s saw the first provision of municipal flats and suburban housing for the poor. However, this resulted in many poor people losing their homes when the slums were cleared to provide the new housing. By 1912, the London County Council had displaced nearly half as many people as it re-housed.

It was the rise of the middle classes that brought about the greatest change and had the most dramatic effect on housing. From 1881 to 1911, another million people were employed in middle- or lower-middle-class jobs. What the new class of consumers wanted were affordable and manageable-sized homes within commuting distance of their work in the cities and towns. Flats were one possibility. Home-making manuals from 1900 to 1920 carried articles on the advantages and disadvantages of flats and maisonettes and recommended how to furnish them and accommodate servants in them. However, the majority of middle-class people still preferred a house, but these only became affordable when, in 1904, the Secretary of the Halifax Building Society offered mortgages of up to 90 percent on homes valued at less than £200.

(Adapted from Hockman 1998)

TASK 3

Look at the biographical information below on Nelson Mandela. Use this information to construct a paragraph about his life. Try to use some of the chronological words and phrases listed above and reorganize any of the information where helpful. Write your paragraph in the past tense.

1918 – Nelson Mandela is born in a small village in South Africa's Eastern Cape.
1919 – His father is dispossessed on the orders of a white magistrate, losing most of his cattle, land and income.

1927 – His father dies.
1927 – With the death of his father, he is placed in care.
1943 – Joins the African National Congress (ANC), initially as an activist.
1944 – With close friends Oliver Tambo and Walter Sislu, he forms the Youth League of the ANC.
1944 – Marries his first wife, Evelyn Mase.
1956 – Mandela is accused of conspiring to overthrow the South African state by violent means, and is charged with high treason. The charges are dropped after a four-year trial.
1957 – Divorces Evelyn Mase.
1958 – Marries Winnie Madikizela.
1960 – The ANC is banned and Mandela forms an underground military wing.
1964 – Captured by police after more than a year on the run, he is convicted of sabotage and treason in June and sentenced to life imprisonment.
1980 – an international campaign for his release launched.
1990 – Mandela is released from prison.
1993 – Mandela awarded the Nobel Peace Prize.
1994 – Mandela elected President.

    TASK KEY

TASK 1   (Possible answer)

There are six main steps involved in making a film: finding a property, writing a script, casting, filming, editing, and composing the music to accompany the film.

First, a suitable 'property' needs to be found. This is the story on which the film is to be based, and it may be original or an adaptation of an existing story.

Once a property has been chosen a script then needs to be written. This is a lengthy and time-consuming task which is normally done by either the original writer or by the director. Even when done by the original writer, the director and producer usually remain closely involved in the production of the script.

After the script is completed, the process begins of casting actors and actresses to star in the film. These may be big international movie stars or more obscure individuals who have yet to make a name for themselves in the industry.

Casting is followed by filming, which can normally take anything from six to eight months and is typically non-chronological. Filming takes place either on soundstages or on location, the latter usually being extremely expensive.

Once filming is complete and the director satisfied with the results, the process of editing the film gets underway. This is a long and complicated process as the editor must ensure that only the best takes are selected, the scenes are an appropriate length, and that the overall pacing of the film is correct.

The final step in making a film is the composition of the music, sometimes called the 'score'. The composer is generally called in after the editing process is complete and needs to be skilled at simultaneously watching the film and composing the music for it. Once he has completed his work, both the director and producer must approve the soundtrack to the film.

TASK 2   (Possible answer)

A typical hairdryer consists of a heating coil, a simple motor-driven fan and a barrel.

In a conventional hairdryer, electrical energy is transformed into convective heat. When the hairdryer is plugged in and switched on, current flows through the circuit which directs power to both the coiled wire of the heating element and the small electric motor. The heating element becomes hot and the electric motor spins, thereby turning the fan.

In order for the airflow generated by the fan to be heated, it needs to be directed down the barrel and over and through the heating element, where it is warmed by the element coil via a process of forced convection. Once heated, it streams out the end of the barrel.

TASK 3   (Possible answer)

Nelson Mandela was born in 1918 in a small village in South Africa's Eastern Cape. A year later, his father was dispossessed on the orders of a white magistrate and lost most of his cattle, land and income. He eventually died in 1927 and Mandela was subsequently placed in care. At the age of 25 he joined the African national Congress (ANC) as an activist and in the following year (1944) formed the Youth League of the ANC with his close friends Oliver Tambo and Walter Sislu. That same year, he married his first wife, Evelyn Mase, whom he subsequently divorced in 1957. He would marry his second wife, Winnie Madikizela, only one year later. After being accused of conspiring to overthrow the South African state by violent means in 1956, the charges against him were dropped following a four-year trial. The ANC was banned in 1960, yet Mandela went on to form an underground military wing, only to be captured four years later after having been on the run. He was convicted of sabotage and treason in June 1964 and sentenced to life imprisonment. As a result of an international campaign for his release, launched in 1980, Nelson Mandela was eventually released in 1990. He went to receive the Nobel Peace prize and to become President in 1993 and 1994 respectively. He is now widely regarded as one of the greatest of all statesmen.

1.4 Comparing and contrasting

Comparison and contrast involves consideration of the similarities and differences between two or more things.

It is important to remember that the word comparison *can itself mean discussing both similarities* and/or *differences. As such, when a question asks you to 'Compare X and Y in terms of . . .', you are expected to compare* and *contrast X and Y.*

There are three methods that can be used when comparing and contrasting:

1.4.1 Method 1: Point-by-point comparison

This is where a particular point relating to Item 1 is analysed and then compared or contrasted with Item 2. If there is more than one point of comparison, each is dealt with and compared in turn. This is the best method to use if you have more than two or three points of comparison as grouping together all the similarities or differences between two or more items makes for easier reading.

Point A of Item 1
Point A of Item 2
Point B of Item 1
Point B of Item 2 . . . and so on.

Example

Private law is concerned with the legal relationships of ordinary persons in everyday transactions (Point A Item 1). Public law, on the other hand, is concerned with the constitution and functions of various kinds of governmental organisations and their legal relationship with the citizen and each other (Point A Item 2). Private law includes contract and commercial law, the law of tort and laws relating to property and the family (Point B Item 1) as opposed to crime, which is the concern of public law (Point B Item 2). A further division, civil law, includes both private and public law with the exception of criminal law.

(Adapted from Keenan 2004)

1.4.2 Method 2: Similarities and differences comparison

Here, either all the similarities between each item are discussed first, followed by the differences, or all the differences between each item are discussed first, followed by the similarities. Whether you choose to discuss similarities or differences first will often depend on which of the two you wish to place greater emphasis. Sometimes, an item will receive greater emphasis if it is placed first; however, there are occasions when placing an item last can give it greater emphasis, particularly if it is being used as a stepping-off point for the next sentence or idea. Also, an item placed last can receive greater prominence simply because readers often better remember the material which is freshest in their minds.

Similarities between items 1 and 2
Point A
Point B
Point C . . . and so on.

Differences between items 1 and 2
Point A
Point B
Point C . . . and so on.

Example

Spermatophytes, a major group of seed producing plants, can be divided into two sub-groups called angiosperms and gymnosperms. The former comprises all flowering plants and most plants fall within this group while most gymnosperms are conifers, the majority of which produce cones, not flowers.

These two sub-groups have a number of similarities and differences, but it is their similarities that enable them to be classified under the same major group. They are similar in that they both have a dominant sporophyte, a reduced gametophyte, and male and female spores. The embryo sacs of plants in both groups are enclosed in ovules and when fertilized the embryo sac develops into a seed.

At this point the two sub-groups differ. Angiosperms produce seeds protected within an ovary and the ovary wall develops into a fruit, while gymnosperms produce seeds which are not protected in this way, and they do not produce fruit. For this reason, the word 'gymnosperm' means 'naked seed'. Unlike in gymnosperms, a style and stigma and companion cells are present in angiosperms and they can be further subdivided into monocotyledons and dicotyledons.

1.4.3 Method 3: Item-by-item comparison

In this case, various points relating to item 1 are discussed in a 'block' of text which may comprise one or more paragraphs. These same points are then discussed in relation to item 2, in a second block of text in which comparisons are highlighted explicitly or implicitly. Arguably, this method has the advantage of being the least complex, although some would say that it is less effective at emphasizing similarities or differences because the different points of comparison between the items concerned are not discussed 'side by side' in the same block of text.

> Item 1
> Point A
> Point B
> Point C
>
> Item 2
> Point A
> Point B
> Point C

Example

Look at the following comparison of two artistic movements using Method 3. Notice how, in order to emphasize the differences between the two movements, contrastive words and phrases have been used in the second paragraph:

> Both Neoclassicism and Romanticism were dominant movements in European art and architecture from around 1750 to 1850. Neoclassicism was an austere art, which showed a return to original classical models, especially those of classical Rome. However, it was not just the 'style' of ancient Rome that served as a model, but also the ideals of Republican Rome. Therefore, Neoclassicism has moral as well as aesthetic implications, particularly in France where the ideals of Republican Rome reflected those of revolutionary Republican France. Neoclassicism is also seen as mounting a reaction against the decadence and frivolity of the Rococo style.
>
> Unlike Neoclassicism, Romanticism had no unity of style or formality. In contrast to Neoclassicism, Romanticism believed in the importance of individual independence and personal (and therefore) subjective expression. Consequently, it was not governed by rules or uniformity of style, as was Neoclassicism. What clearly distinguishes Romanticism from Neoclassicism is opposition to the use of models from the past and its concentration upon content rather than form.
>
> The differences between Neoclassicism and Romanticism can be summed up as a concern with classical line, form and balance on the one hand, and colour, ideas and dynamism on the other.

It is possible to make the differences between two items clear by implication. In other words, by describing those characteristics that apply to item 1, we can imply that they do not apply to item 2, without having to say so directly. Look at the following example:

Example

It is necessary to make clear the difference between a navigable river and a canal. There are really two differences, the first of which is legal. A river is a natural phenomenon, which is subject to legal claims for purposes other than navigation – water supply, boundaries, fords, and fishing. The second difference is physical. A river does not have to be artificially supplied with water.

(Adapted from Harvie 1972)

From what is actually stated here, we can assume that a canal (in contrast to a river) is *only* used for navigation and that it *does* have to be artificially supplied with water. However, you will notice that this is not stated directly. By using implication in this way, we can reduce our writing load. Be careful though: you cannot always rely on implication and may need to be more explicit! As usual, put yourself in the reader's shoes and ask yourself the question, 'Would I be able to draw the correct inference from what I have written?'

1.4.4 Words and phrases associated with comparison and contrast

Showing similarity

> *Similarly, . . .*
> *In the same way, . . .*
> *Likewise, . . .*
> *Correspondingly, . . .*
> *X is similar to Y in that both demonstrate . . .*
> *X is very much like Y in that both display . . .*
> *X shows similar characteristics to Y in that they both . . .*
> *X and Y have several characteristics (features) in common. These include . . .*
> *There are several similarities between X and Y*
> *Both X and Y are . . .*
> *Neither X nor Y is/are . . .*
> *Both . . ., but neither . . .*

Showing dissimilarity

> *In contrast (to)*
> *There are marked differences between . . .*
> *What clearly distinguishes X from Y is . . .*
> *Conditions in/relating to X are/were different from those . . .*
> *Unlike in science, where the term has a universally agreed definition, its use in economics is open to a number of interpretations.*
> *. . . Comparing like with like . . .*
> *. . . of greater/lesser significance than . . .*
> *Whilst/Although X is . . ., Y is . . .*
> *X may, on balance, be more likely than Y to . . .*

Indicating limitations of a comparison

> *Any comparison between X and Y must necessarily be of limited value/ validity . . .*
> *This comparison must be viewed with a degree of caution . . .*
> *Comparisons between X and Y are possible only as far as . . . is/are concerned.*
> *The extent to which X and Y can be compared (very much) depends on . . .*
> *The extent to which a comparison can be made between X and Y is dependent upon . . .*

TASK 1

Compare and contrast two closely related terms used in your field in order to show their similarities and differences:

Example   Term a: *computer*   Term b: *word processor*

A computer is a device that *is similar to* a word processor *in that* it can be used to produce and edit text; however, it *differs from* a word processor *in that* it can be programmed and can be used for other applications, such as spreadsheets and databases.

---

1. Term a: Term b:

Sentence: _____

_____

_____

2. Term a: Term b:

Sentence: _____

             _____

             _____

TASK 2

Compare and contrast the main soil types described below, reorganizing the information and dividing your writing into paragraphs where necessary. Use appropriate comparison and contrast linking words and phrases and try to begin with a short introductory sentence or paragraph.

PEATY

Appearance: dark
Texture: soft, spongy
Features: high organic content, acidic, easily worked, retains moisture

CHALKY

Appearance: grey
Texture: dry, crumbly, white chalk pieces
Features: alkaline, free-draining, few nutrients

SANDY

Appearance: light, orangey-brown
Texture: gritty
Features: free-draining, few nutrients, warms up quickly, very dry in warm weather

CLAY

Appearance: medium brown
Texture: heavy, sticky when wet and solid lumps when dry
Features: poor drainage, good nutrient retention, cold – slow to warm up, heavy to work, cracks on surface in dry weather, waterlogged in wet weather, particularly in winter

SILT

Appearance: dark
Texture: smooth, silky
Features: drainage quite good, easy to work

TASK 3

Following is some information comparing and contrasting asexual and sexual reproduction in plants. Match the items in the left-hand column with those in the right and note the language used to compare and contrast.

---

1. *What clearly distinguishes* asexual *from* sexual reproduction in plants . . .

2. The advantage of this is that . . .

3. *However*, the disadvantage is that . . .

4. *Compared with* sexual reproduction . . .

5. *On the other hand*, if plants overbreed . . .

6. Almost all plants reproduce sexually; . . .

a) a species is therefore more susceptible to being wiped out by disease

b) they can become incapable of sexual reproduction and asexual reproduction then needs to take place

c) growth is more rapid in plants reproduced asexually

d) is that with the former, the new plant is genetically identical to the parent

e) this produces new varieties which improve a species' survival rate

f) the new plant is identical in appearance as it shares the same genes as the original

---

TASK 4

Use the following information to compare and contrast the legal system of England and Wales with that of Scotland. Decide which method of comparison (see above) is the most suitable for this task and use appropriate link words.

Legal system of England and Wales

- Termed English law;
- Basis of other common law legal systems including Commonwealth;
- Originates from 12th century in reign of Henry II;
- Based on precedent (previous decisions of judges in court cases);
- Common law can be amended/repealed by Parliament of the United Kingdom.

Legal System of Scotland

- Based on 6th century Roman law – result of introduction of Canon Law – similar to that of continental Europe;
- Pluralistic legal system – mix of uncodified civil law and common law;

- Influence of English law after Acts of Union (1707);
- 1998 – Scottish Parliament – makes laws within powers granted by Westminster Parliament for certain areas (e.g. health, education);
- Laws relating to some areas common to both jurisdictions – England & Wales and Scotland (e.g. consumer law).

 TASK KEY

TASK 2 (Possible answer)

There are a number of different soil types and for the successful cultivation of vegetables and plants commercial growers and gardeners should ascertain the type of soil with which they are working. One easy way to do this is to check the appearance and texture of the soil; these will provide a strong indication of the soil type. For a more scientific analysis, soil analysis kits are available.

The soils with the darkest appearance tend to be peaty or silty soils. Peaty soils have a soft, spongy texture when squeezed *while* silty soils have a smoother and more silky feel. Peaty soils are particularly good for retaining moisture – an important feature in hot, dry weather, but, *on the other hand*, they have a tendency to retain too much moisture in very wet conditions. *Both* peat and silt, *unlike* clay, are easy to work; *however*, peat, due to its high organic content, is very acidic, which means that it is not suitable for all plants and most vegetables. Peaty soil is also low in nutrients, so it requires the addition of fertilizers. Silty soil, on the other hand, is very fertile and has good moisture retention.

Both chalky and sandy soils are easy to identify because the former is light brown in colour and has a dry, crumbly texture with white chalk pieces present, while the latter is orangey brown with a very gritty texture. They are *both* very low in nutrients and free draining, so they dry out in summer; they are considered to be poor soils requiring the addition of fertilizers and other soil improvers to maintain healthy growth. The advantage of a sandy soil is that it warms up quickly, so encourages early plant growth. Chalky soil is very alkaline; it is, therefore not a suitable growing medium for a large number of plants.

Clay and loamy soils are medium brown in colour, but soils with a very high clay content can appear more grey. Clay soils can be quite difficult to work because they are heavy and sticky in wet conditions due to poor drainage – this can lead to the soil being waterlogged and unworkable in very wet periods – but in dry weather cracks appear on the surface and when dug, the soil forms hard, solid lumps that require considerable effort to break up. *On the other hand*, clay soils have good nutrient retention, but, *unlike* sand, they are cold soils, which are very slow to warm up, so do not promote early plant growth. Loamy soil is considered to be the best of all soil types because it is a combination of sand, silt and clay, which, when combined, give it a high nutrient content and good drainage but sufficient moisture retention for good plant growth. It is also generally easy to work with the exception of some loams, which, like clay, may be heavier to work.

TASK 3

1. d
2. f
3. a
4. c
5. b
6. e

TASK 4   (Possible answer)

The legal system of England and Wales (termed 'English law'), unlike that of Scotland, forms the basis of common law legal systems in many other countries, including those of the Commonwealth. English law originates from the reign of Henry II in the 12th century. English common law is shaped by judges who employ legal precedent when making decisions in court.

The Scottish legal system, *in contrast*, is a pluralistic system based on a mix of 6th-century Roman law (civil law) and common law. After the Acts of Union in 1707, English law began to influence Scottish law in certain areas; in 1998 the Scottish Parliament was granted law-making powers in areas such as health and education. Nowadays, laws exist which are common to both jurisdictions, most notably consumer law.

1.5 Classifying

The process of classification helps you to organize your writing by classifying items into clearly identifiable groups. This allows you to break down your topic into more manageable chunks and to deal with each chunk in the most logical order (see Section 2.1).

Classifying concepts or physical objects/phenomena into groups allows you to define them more clearly and to highlight their similarities and differences. This can be seen in the biological world, for example, where the plant and animal kingdoms are divided into different classes – the major classification of the animal kingdom being vertebrates and invertebrates, with vertebrates being further divided into sub-groups, namely fish, amphibians, reptiles, birds and mammals. Similarly, in the world of marketing, the population is divided into different groups called 'segments', and products are then designed specifically with one or more particular segments of the market in mind. Such market divisions can be made on the basis of gender, age, geographical location, or socio-economic group.

Example

Rainfall can be classified into three types. The first type is cyclonic rain, which is caused by warm air being undercut by colder air. The second type is convectional rainfall, caused by air warmed by the hot earth rising and cooling as it meets colder layers. The final type of rainfall is relief (orographic) rainfall, which is caused by moist air being cooled as it is forced to rise up the sides of hills or mountains.

Classification of Rainfall

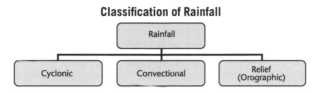

Example

Horticulturalists group plants into genera, species and families. The genus name represents a group of plants with similar characteristics: these are plants with a common evolutionary ancestor. The species name represents a sub-group of one or more plants within the genus; again, these are plants with similar characteristics and plants within the same species can reproduce with each other. Within a species there can be variations which need to be separately identified. Both the genus name and species name are in Latin and many common names, which are those known and used by most people to refer to a plant, are the same as the genus name: for example, clematis and hydrangea. The relationship between genus and species is often shown in the form of a family tree. The final and highest grouping is family. All plants belong to a family and all plants within a family share common characteristics; one family can be made up of a number of genera. The family name is not necessary to make the plant name unique, so it is not written as part of the plant name. To illustrate, the poppy is in a family called Papaveraceae. It belongs to the genus Papaver and one species is orientale. One example of a cultivated variety (cultivar) of poppy is 'Mrs Perry'.

(Adapted from Dawson 1994)

Classification of the Poppy Family

```
                    Papaveraceae
                      (Family)

                       Papaver
                       (Genus)

   P. nudicaule       P. orientale              P. somniferum
    (Species)          (Species)                  (Species)

'Champagne Bubbles'  'Mrs Perry'  'May Queen'   'Pink Beauty'  'White Cloud'
    (Cultivar)       (Cultivar)   (Cultivar)     (Cultivar)     (Cultivar)
```

Example

> Volcanoes are the most common landform that result from extrusive volcanic
> activity and they may be classified in a number of ways: according to the
> characteristics of the extruded material (acidic or basic), the nature of the
> opening or vent through which the lava emerges (fissure or vent), the
> frequency of the eruption in a particular location (regular or infrequent) and
> the degree of violence of the eruption (explosive or gentle). These factors
> determine the shapes and sizes of volcanoes.
>
> (Pearson Education 2001: 6)

Classification of Volcanoes

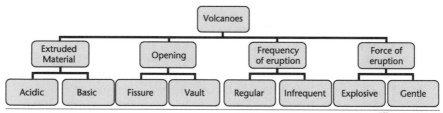

```
                            Volcanoes

   Extruded         Opening         Frequency          Force of
   Material                        of eruption         eruption

 Acidic   Basic   Fissure  Vault  Regular  Infrequent  Explosive  Gentle
```

*Because classification follows the kind of tree-like structure
illustrated above, such diagrams can be a very useful way
of creating an outline for your material before you begin
writing.*

1.5.1 Words and phrases associated with classification

X can be analysed/broken down into three types.
X can be categorised/classified/grouped according to . . .
The first/second/third/next/final or last type/kind/category/division is made up of/
*   comprises . . .*
One type . . .

Another type . . .
Still/yet another type is . . .

TASK 1

Note: You may like to try drawing a tree diagram before you begin writing.

a) Write an introduction by combining the following four sentences into two.

Spermatophytes are a major group of plants.
They are all seed-producing plants.
Angiosperms and gymnosperms are subdivisions.
Angiosperms produce flowers and most gymnosperms are conifers, and the majority produce cones.

---

b) Now write a second paragraph explaining the features that allow the latter two groups to be classified under the same major group. Use the language of comparison (see Section 1.4) and appropriate link words:

They have certain similarities:

• a dominant sporophyte;
• a reduced gametophyte;
• separate male (pollen grains) and female (embryo sac) spores = heterosporous;
• the embryo sac is enclosed in an ovule;
• the fertilized embryo sac develops into a seed;
• a pollen tube is present.

---

c) Write a third paragraph explaining why angiosperms and gymnosperms are divided into two separate sub groups. Use the language of contrast (see Section 1.4) and appropriate link words to connect your points.

They have certain differences:

Angiosperms

• produce seeds within an ovary;
• ovary wall develops into a fruit;

- fruits formed after fertilization;
- style and stigma present;
- companion cells present;
- sub-groups: monocotyledons (cotyledon = 'leaf'), one seed leaf within seed (e.g. grasses, tulips, daffodils), and dicotyledons, two seed leaves within seed (e.g. most trees and shrubs).

Gymnosperms (name = 'naked seed') have none of the above

Having completed this task, you will have employed the functions of comparison and contrast and classification (see Sections 1.4 and 1.5) in the organization of your writing.

---

d) Look at the introductory paragraph of the classification framework given above. Answer the following questions:

- What is the purpose of the first two sentences given?
- What function do the next two sentences perform?

TASK 2

Take an item from your subject area. Prepare a tree diagram placing the item in a general class. Then divide the general class into two or more sub-classes. Are any further divisions of these sub-classes possible? If so, add these to your tree diagram. Now use your tree diagram to write a short essay using Task #1 as a model.

  TASK KEY

TASK 1 (Possible answers)

a) Spermatophytes are a major group of plants, all of which produce seeds and can be divided into one of two sub-groups called angiosperms and gymnosperms. The former comprises all flowering plants and most plants fall within this group, while most gymnosperms are conifers, the majority of which produce cones rather than flowers.

b) These two sub-groups can be classified under the same major group because they have a number of characteristics in common. They are similar in that they both have a dominant sporophyte and a reduced gametophyte.

They are both heterosporous, which means they have male (pollen grains) and female (embryo sac) spores. The embryo sacs are enclosed in ovules and when fertilized the embryo sac develops into a seed. Plants in both groups also have pollen tubes.

c) Despite these similarities, there are also a number of differences between the two sub-groups. Angiosperms produce seeds within an ovary and the ovary wall develops into a fruit, while gymnosperms produce seeds which are not protected within an ovary, and they do not produce fruit. For this reason, the word 'gymnosperm' means 'naked seed'.

Unlike in gymnosperms, a style and stigma and companion cells are present in angiosperms. A final difference is that angiosperms can be further subdivided into monocotyledons and dicotyledons. A 'cotyledon' is a leaf: monocotyledons have one seed leaf within their seed whereas dicotyledons have two. Monocots include grasses and ornamental plants like tulips and daffodils, and Dicots include most trees and shrubs.

d) i. The introductory sentences aim to place the items to be described into a general class – spermatophytes.

ii. They set up the basis for the classification by dividing the general class into two sub-classes: angiosperms and gymnosperms and indicate the major difference between the two.

1.6 Explaining causes and effects

The discussion of causal relationships is common in academic writing where it is often necessary to understand and explain the reasons why things happen, to justify why certain decisions have been taken (in the design of methodology, for example), or to interpret data.

In order to present causes and/or effects clearly to your reader, you can either

- discuss all the causes first and then discuss the effects in separate paragraphs. Once you have discussed the causes, you may wish to summarize these in a separate paragraph before discussing the effects. This summary will act as a link, thereby helping to improve the flow of your writing – see also Section 2.2;
- mention each cause separately and then discuss its effect(s) in the same or the following paragraph; or
- group different causes/effects that share certain characteristics, then deal with each group in turn.

Whichever approach you choose, it is important that you explain it to the reader in order to prepare them and help them navigate more easily through your discussion.

As we have seen, in any extended writing different functions can be simultaneously employed to help you organize your material more effectively. For example, classification (see Section 1.5) could be used to group different categories of causes or effects; thus, in order to answer the question, '*What effects have various new technologies had on present-day society?*', you could classify the different areas of life where new technologies have been introduced and then examine their impact upon each area (e.g. in the workplace, in the home, in the fields of education, medicine, etc.). Embedding one form of organization within another in this way creates textual depth or richness and can help give much needed structure to your written work.

Example

What follows is a description of the effects of the transition from a rural to an urban society that occurred in Western Europe; a transition caused by the Industrial Revolution:

> The Industrial Revolution changed Western Europe from a predominantly rural to a predominantly urban society; this had a number of important effects. A population concentrated in cities was more accessible to the influence of new ideological trends than a population scattered through the countryside. This led to the city becoming the breeding ground of nationalist and socialist doctrines, of new religious sects, temperance societies, reform movements, and revolutionary associations. It was also the city that gave birth in the late nineteenth century to the cheap daily newspaper, which thereafter helped mould public opinion on political and social issues. The revolutions of 1848 were a further consequence of the move from country to towns. The towns experienced a declining standard of life and a phase of acute hardship and unemployment. The conditions bred the revolutionary spirit and provided the numbers of concentration and strength which a revolutionary movement needed in order to challenge established authority.
>
> (Adapted from Gilbert and Clay 1991; Thomson 1990)

1.6.1 Words and phrases associated with cause and effect

Showing causes

because/since/as/due to . . .
X is a/the cause of . . .
X is a causal factor in . . .
X determines whether . . .
As a result of X; because of X

Showing effects

accordingly
hence/thus/therefore/consequently
for this reason
X led to . . .
Because of this,

Because of this/because of the fact that . . .	*X had an effect on/led to* *X results in/has resulted in/ has led to/has contributed to . . .* *X is a result/consequence of . . .* *From this, it follows that . . .* *X is a consequence of . . .* *Resulting from this . . .* *. . . resulting in/from . . .*

TASK 1

Combine the following sentences to form a complete paragraph explaining why an area of coastline in Southern England collapsed in 1999. Where appropriate, try to use some of the cause–effect phrases highlighted earlier:

- the weather had been very dry for 30 months;
- the cliffs became brittle;
- there was then above-average rainfall for 8 of the 12 months preceding the collapse;
- the cliffs became waterlogged and soggy;
- the weather turned cold;
- the water in the rock froze;
- when water freezes it expands;
- this, along with erosion from the sea, made the cliff crumble.

TASK 2

What follows are some notes for an essay explaining the possible causes of an increase in juvenile crime. The introduction and conclusion have been written for you; use the notes given for each of the paragraphs to write complete sentences. Try to expand the information given, providing further details to support each of the points made. Use cause and effect words and phrases where appropriate.

Increasing levels of juvenile crime is an area of great concern in Britain today. While it is true that serious crime involving young offenders is not a new phenomenon – the case of Jamie Bulger in the early 1990s is a stark example – it is the increasing incidence and severity of crimes committed by teenagers which is worrying both parents and the authorities. This has led to some sections of the media adopting the term 'feral children', thereby implying that society is under threat from groups of young people who are out of control. In order to determine the roots of this problem, it is necessary to examine three main areas in an attempt to pinpoint the causes of antisocial and criminal behaviour.

The first area to examine is the home . . .

(**Notes:** Increased family breakdown – dysfunctional family environment – no good role models for children, particularly males – often no father figure present – lack of parental discipline – children not taught moral values – little interaction with adults, only with their peers whose values and norms of behaviour may be skewed – do not learn to respect adults, including the elderly in society = no sense of responsibility.)

Violence, portrayed on a daily basis on television, on the internet and in increasingly violent video games, is another contributory factor to higher crime rates involving extreme violence amongst teenagers.

(**Notes:** Viewing such material regularly – desensitization of the young – act out their fantasies – lack of empathy with victims – psychopathic tendencies – desire to win 'respect' of peers, particularly gang members – gratuitous violence – availability of weapons, guns, knives.)

A third area under scrutiny is the development of a materialistic society where what an individual 'owns' is more important than the intangible qualities he or she possesses . . .

(**Notes:** Celebrity culture – success measured in terms of money and the things it can buy – designer items, certain types of cars, etc. – desire for expensive consumer goods – latest mobile phones, etc. – obtain by theft involving violent attacks? – possessions = power = success = respect of peers – lethal combination, particularly among non- or low-wage earners.)

An examination of each of these areas leads to the conclusion that society is suffering from a lack of cohesion and a lack of strong moral values, which can only be inculcated in the home and reinforced in the education system. These problems, together with a desire for increasingly high-value material possessions fuelled by a vacuous, superficial celebrity culture, are at the root of the malaise found among young people in some sections of society. These areas need to be urgently addressed if a further downward spiral of antisocial behaviour among the young is to be prevented.

 TASK KEY

TASK 1   (Possible answer)

In the late 1990s, the southern coast of England experienced a very dry spell of weather extending over a period of 30 weeks. As a result, the cliffs became very brittle. Following this dry spell, the same coastline experienced above-average rainfall for 8 of the 12 months preceding the collapse, causing the cliffs to become waterlogged and soggy. The weather then turned cold, which in turn led to the water in the rock freezing and subsequently expanding.

Because of this, the rock crumbled and the cliff face collapsed. The destruction of the coastline was consequently the result of a combination of weather extremes and erosion from the sea.

TASK 2 (Possible answer)

The first area to examine is the home. An increased incidence of family breakdown as a result of parents splitting up, or unmarried mothers bearing children from a number of different fathers, has led to many children being brought up in a dysfunctional family environment. This means that often there is no father figure present to act as an effective role model and instil discipline, particularly for male children. Another problem is that nowadays many children are not taught strict moral values; consequently, they do not learn to respect others in society and do not learn what is acceptable behaviour and what is not. Because many youngsters have little interaction with adults in the home, and instead spend large amounts of time either alone in front of a computer or socializing with their peers, their values and norms of behaviour may become skewed. This can lead to feelings of alienation from adult society, a general sense of detachment and a lack of respect for the elderly – all fuelled by an inadequately developed sense of responsibility.

Violence, portrayed on a daily basis on television, on the internet and in increasingly violent video games, is another contributory factor to higher crime rates involving extreme violence among teenagers. Viewing such material regularly desensitizes the young, some of whom act out their fantasies. Psychopathic tendencies can develop in some youngsters, with a distinct lack of empathy with their victims becoming evident in many cases. There is also an increasing tendency for some young people in inner-city areas to become members of gangs that roam the streets indulging in gratuitous acts of violence in an attempt to win the 'respect' of their peers. This, coupled with the ready availability of various weapons, particularly guns and knives, is an explosive mix, which has seen crime levels in many cities escalate in the last five years.

A third area under scrutiny is the development of a materialistic society where what an individual 'owns' is more important than the intangible qualities that he or she possesses. We live in a 'celebrity culture', where success is measured in terms of money and the things it can buy; these usually include the latest mobile phones, a variety of designer labels and expensive, high-performance cars. Naturally, young people also want to own these items, but unlike the celebrities they admire, they are unable to afford them; consequently, some resort to theft – behaviour that sometimes involves violent attacks upon unsuspecting victims. The motivation for this behaviour is clear: for these young people, owning the latest expensive consumer goods elevates them to a position of power and earns them the respect of their peers, who also see this as the path to 'success'. This is a lethal combination.

1.7 Developing an argument

Argument is perhaps the most important and most difficult function to master. Although there are guides, such as this one, that provide pointers to the basic principles underlying an effective, well-structured argument, the skill of honing an argument is one which is developed over time through practice, the receipt of feedback, and reading the eloquent expositions of other, successful writers. Nevertheless, let us look here at some key issues.

Good argument requires at least the following inter-related elements:

- a clear structure and focus;
- sound logic;
- the presentation of robust evidence;
- the effective use of appropriate link words and phrases to introduce and connect your ideas.

Another key requirement when constructing a good argument is the ability to adopt and express a critical and objective outlook and to have a personal perspective or view on what it is you are analysing and discussing. This can often be difficult for students who feel uneasy about questioning the views of published authors or their professors; nevertheless, as we shall see in Section 5.14, the need to 'find your own voice' and the confidence required to do so remains a fundamental part of higher education culture in the UK and many other parts of the world, and in particular during the research process, where students are expected to go beyond simply reproducing the ideas of others. Suffice it to say that so long as you keep in mind the key elements of good argument listed above, you should not go far wrong.

Logical argument supported by robust evidence forms the basis of good academic writing. Such evidence may take the form of *a-priori* truths, sound and detailed rationales, reliable data, or the word of well-recognized and respected authorities in the field. When writing your assignment or research report you must keep sight of the need to convince those who read it that any claims it makes are well founded. The way to do this is by offering them convincing reasons, in the form of reliable evidence, why they should accept those claims. Generally speaking, the stronger the claim you make, the weightier the supporting evidence for it needs to be. Be careful not to make claims your evidence is not robust enough to support (see Section 4.7).

1.7.1 Making a claim

One way of making a claim is first to highlight a 'problem' or point of contention to which your essay or research offers a new perspective or 'solution'. For example, you may wish to claim that a widely held belief is 'questionable', 'flawed', 'misguided' or simply 'incorrect'. In the process of articulating that belief you may well use phrases such as *It has been claimed/ argued that . . ., Some writers have claimed that . . ., It is the view of some researchers that . . .*, or *It is often/sometimes argued/said that. . . .* Each of these phrases can serve as a preface or stepping-stone to calling into question a particular claim made by other scholars (for more information see Section 6.7, Literature Review).

Having identified a problem, the next step is to propose a solution (comprising one or more claims) along with supporting evidence. You may wish here to state explicitly your line of argument using phrases such as *It is here argued that . . .* or *In what follows it is argued that . . ., The stance adopted in the following pages is . . .*

1.7.2 Structuring your argument

Although your arguments may have the support of logic and sound evidence, they nevertheless need to be presented in a way that makes them easily accessible to the reader so that the underlying logic is apparent. In other words, your arguments need to be well structured (see Coherence, Section 2.1).

The way in which you structure your argument will in part depend on your research topic. For some research topics (most notably, but not solely, in the sciences), inductive reasoning, which often involves using evidence from observation to support a general conclusion, is commonly employed. In other disciplines, argument is often expressed deductively – here, known facts are used to 'dictate' a particular conclusion. However, whichever form of reasoning is used, argument in any discipline is a form of persuasion; you should think of the argument within your essay or research report as a 'debate' with fellow students, only with you taking on all roles: you will need to express your personal view, but also present the opinions of others so that, where necessary, you can subsequently offer evidence of your own that either totally or partially refutes those opinions. To extend the debate metaphor further, you have the difficult job of acting as both chairman and participants in the debate and at all times you must keep your eye on the ball to ensure that your argument

- addresses others' shortcomings;
- anticipates and deflects all potential criticisms as far as possible;
- is focused;
- is clearly expressed;
- is well supported.

All argument in academic writing should make an appeal to reason rather than emotion. Emotive words or statements are inappropriate in an academic context as they make your writing sound subjective when all academic argument should be as objective as possible; you should therefore aim for a neutral tone.

1.7.3 Inductive and deductive reasoning

As we have seen, there are two ways in which an argument can be developed. The first uses inductive reasoning where specific evidence is offered in support of a general conclusion. What follows is an example of inductive argumentation.

Example

> Most people would agree with the proposition that smoking is a harmful leisure activity, for statistics prove this to be the case. What is not so clear, however, is that passive smoking may be as harmful to those who are regularly exposed to the smoke of others. Various studies indicate that regularly inhaling 'second-hand' smoke can damage your health. Compared to non-smokers who live and work in a smoke-free environment, those non-smokers who do not work in such an environment are statistically more likely to develop lung cancer and other smoking-related diseases. As a result of these findings, there is an EU-wide initiative to ban smoking in restaurants and bars; such a ban has recently come into effect in the UK and the Republic of Ireland.

Deductive argumentation usually takes the form of a syllogism, where the stated premises (reasons given) provide logical grounds for the conclusion. The simplest syllogism contains two premises and a conclusion that follows from them. For example:

1. All English people are unfriendly.
2. Peter is English.
3. Therefore, Peter is unfriendly.

In a syllogism, if the major premise (1) and the minor premise (2) are true, the conclusion (3) will be true because it follows logically from both preceding premises: if 1 and 2 are valid, then logically 3 must also be valid. However, logical validity is not the same as empirical truth. Because premise 1 is false (not *all* English people are unfriendly), then conclusion (3) is invalid. Therefore, in deductive reasoning, there is a strong relationship between premises and conclusion: to present a strong argument with a valid conclusion, the premises on which that conclusion rests must themselves be valid.

Complex arguments involve a chain of interlocking syllogisms – these will probably not be stated as overtly as in the example, but will be present none-theless. If you are trying to refute an argument, you will need to identify and evaluate the truth of its premises and decide whether the conclusion shown to derive from them is logically valid. And, of course, you will need to apply equal rigour to the evaluation of your own arguments if they are not to be vulnerable to criticism from other scholars and examiners.

TASK 1

Look at the extract below by David Henderson and answer the questions that follow:

In all this, there is a common presumption. It is that the existence of large disparities is an evil, and that it gives proof of remediable injustice. It is this belief, in conjunction with the alarmist consensus, that provides the main doctrinal basis for anti-liberalism 2000.

So strong is the presumption of injustice that arguments and evidence to the contrary are often set aside. Consider for example the poor coun-tries that have fallen further behind in recent years. Probably not one of them would now be better off, and some might be worse off, if growth elsewhere in the world had been slower, in which case the gap would have widened less. What really matters is not the gap as such, but the progress of these countries. As to why their recent progress has been so limited, it is clear that in the great majority of cases, perhaps all of them, internal factors have been important if not decisive. Many of the countries have been subject, in different ways, to conflict, disorder and chronic mis-government. In most of these, and in some other countries too, growth has been held back by the economic policies that governments have chosen to pursue . . . It is wrong to present globalisation as a reason why growth has not gone ahead faster in . . . Cuba, North Korea, Afghanistan, Iran, Nigeria, . . . All these obvious facts are played down or disregarded by many commentators because of the wish to portray non-beneficiaries as victims of the system . . . Widening the circle of victims and assigning blame to the operations of 'unfettered' markets point the way to a range of interventionist measures and programmes.

(Henderson 2001: 25–6)

1. What is Henderson's conclusion?
2. List the premises on which his conclusion rests.
3. In the second paragraph, he uses the phrase 'it is clear that . . .' to reinforce his viewpoint. Find two other phrases in the paragraph which perform this function.

TASK 2

One way you can practise the skill of argumentation is to read through a passage that presents a particular argument; this could be a newspaper article or a passage from a textbook or journal article. Try to identify the conclusion and the reasoning behind it. As you read, ask yourself the following questions:

- What is the article/passage trying to persuade me to believe?
- On what grounds is it trying to get me to believe this? (i.e. what is its rationale?)
  Premise 1:
  Premise 2:
  and so on.

Once you have identified the argument put forward and the reasoning behind it, your next task is to evaluate it:

- How valid is each of these premises?
- How valid is the conclusion based on the premises cited?
- Has the writer made any questionable assumptions? For example, has a term been defined in a way that you feel is misleading, erroneous or ambiguous?
- Has the writer made a false analogy, that is, has s/he compared two things on the basis that they are the same when, in fact, they are not?
- How empirically accurate are the reasons and the resulting conclusion? (Remember: there is a distinction between logical validity and empirical truth.)

1.7.4 Words and phrases associated with argumentation

Here are some words and phrases that introduce or act as links between ideas when employing argumentation.

Stating a viewpoint

> *X argues that . . .*
> *X suggests that . . .*
> *An argument often cited in the literature is . . .*
> *X has proposed that . . .*
> *Y develops this argument further by stating that . . .*
> *An alternative view is put forward by Z who states that . . .*
> *P, on the other hand/in contrast, believes that . . .*

Questioning or refuting a viewpoint

Conversely, . . .
It is often stated/said/argued/suggested that . . . However, . . .
Some experts would argue that . . . However, . . .
Some experts/X and Y argue that. . . . Others . . .
Many experts/ agree that . . .
It has long been assumed that . . .
. . . whereas/while . . .
One the one hand . . .; on the other hand, . . .
. . ., yet/but . . .
However, . . .
While . . .
Despite claims that . . .
It is difficult to justify (the view that) . . .
It is/would be difficult to make a strong case/argument for . . .
Another aspect/dimension which may have had a bearing on . . ., and which is/
*   was not taken into consideration/account, is/was . . .*
If X were the case, then Y would be true. That this is not the case suggests that
*   other factors/determinants/issues are involved/are responsible for . . .*
It is an over-simplification to say/state/argue that . . .
If this were so, . . .
X alone is insufficient to explain . . .
It is dangerous to assume that . . .
There is no way of establishing (whether) . . .
X cannot be judged on Y alone.
The success of . . . cannot be attributed to . . .
It is quite wrong to . . .
In itself, X cannot be regarded as evidence/proof of . . .
It is possible to counter such arguments/the argument for . . . by . . .
It is too easy to assume/underestimate the influence/significance of . . .

Refuting a viewpoint by first making a concession:

This argument/view is partially accurate/true; however, . . .
There is some truth/credibility in the argument/in the view that . . .
With one or two exceptions, it would be wrong/incorrect to claim that . . .
This argument has a certain superficial logic, but on closer examination . . .
Whilst it can be argued that . . ., this alone is insufficient to explain . . .
Whilst it is a fact that . . ., it is also true that . . .
It is, of course, possible that . . .; however/on the other hand, it could be argued
*   that . . .*
Although it could be argued that . . . it is also a fact/true/the case that . . .
Even if this assumption holds true, it does not mean that . . .
While it is true that . . ., it must not be forgotten that/it cannot be denied
*   that . . .*
Although it is possible to identify a number of factors that may contribute to . . .,
*   in general their effect on . . . is marginal.*

The ability to cite the views of others is especially useful when writing the Literature Review, Analysis and Discussion, and Conclusion sections of a research report (see Sections 6.7, 6.10 and 6.11).

Stating your own viewpoint

> *It is clear that . . .*
> *It must be accepted that . . .*
> *The evidence indicates that/would appear to suggest that . . .*

It is possible to present two or more opposing views on a topic and to use these as a basis for stating your own view. Following is an example of this approach, where one writer compares and contrasts the views of two well-known authors and then puts forward his own viewpoint on the subject. In so doing, he makes it clear where he agrees and disagrees with the opposing viewpoints:

Example

Both Ashton and Hobsbawn agree that markets for cotton were potentially larger than those for wool and that mechanization was easier in the case of cotton. They further argue that cotton did not have to overcome vested interests in production and control. Where Hobsbawm goes out on his own is in relating the expansion of cotton to the development of slave-worked plantations in the American South. My own view would be to favour Hobsbawm as he takes account of the fall in the cost of raw material as an important factor in increasing production, this being achieved by rapid expansion in cotton cultivation.

(Harvie 1972: 41)

TASK 3

1   Find opinions from two or more sources arguing the same viewpoint on a topic. Paraphrase their views.
2   Find two sources with contrasting viewpoints on the same topic. Paraphrase the opinion of one source then say how the other writer's opinion differs.

TASK 4

Look again at Task #2 in Section 1.6. Do you agree with the viewpoint expressed by the writer concerning the causes of increasing levels of juvenile crime? If yes, write a paragraph in support of that viewpoint. If not, write a paragraph opposing the writer's viewpoint, making clear why you believe the causes given are not valid and suggesting different causes.

 TASK KEY

TASK #1

1. Globalization is not the reason why economic growth in poor countries has been held back.
2. (a) Internal factors are the reason behind the lack of economic progress in these countries.
   (b) Biased commentators wish to portray poor countries as victims of globalisation because they are in favour of interventionist policies – hence they choose to ignore (a), above.
3. What really matters is . . .
   All these obvious facts are . .

2

How should I structure my writing?

2.1 Coherence: the flow of good writing • 2.2 The three main parts of a writing project • 2.3 Citation, referencing and paraphrasing • 2.4 Using footnotes

2.1 Coherence: the flow of good writing

Coherence is perhaps the single most important element in any kind of writing. However, it is particularly crucial in academic writing, where success or failure may well depend upon how clearly you have managed to communicate your ideas and lines of argument to your reader. No matter how insightful or original those ideas may be, if you are not able to present them in a clear and logical way, their meaning and value is lost.

Coherence, then, has to do with arranging your ideas in a way that makes them most easily understood by the reader. A good writer 'sticks' their ideas together so that they act as links in a chain, each link connecting the one before it with the one after. If any links are missing, the connections become unclear and the argument structure breaks down. A well-written essay is rather like an unfolding story, which gradually develops as each block of the tale builds on those that have preceded it. Just as the story has a kind of history, a piece of academic writing has a history in the sequence of ideas that build up its argument structure. The reader is only able to make sense of what he or she is reading at any particular point because it connects clearly with what has gone before, and you the writer must make that connection clear. Figure 2.1 illustrates this.

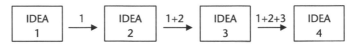

FIGURE 2.1 A sequence of ideas.
(Idea 1 leads into idea 2; ideas 1 and 2 lead into idea 3; ideas 1, 2 and 3 lead into idea 4 etc.)

Unfortunately, it is very easy to assume that because *you* understand what you are writing then your reader will also understand. However, you must remember that you are writing down ideas which are already clear in your own mind, and this means that it is easy for you to miss any incoherence that may exist, because you mentally fill in any gaps automatically. The reader, on the other hand, does not have the knowledge to do this and is therefore often wholly dependent upon what he or she sees on the page. Consequently, when you write down your ideas you must read through them extremely carefully and ask yourself, 'Is this clear to a reader who has no access to the ideas in my head?' It is crucial always to consider your reader(s). One of the main reasons writers fail to make themselves understood is because they take too much for granted and do not connect their ideas together clearly enough. As a result, the reader is unable to make sense of them and is therefore unable to evaluate them favourably.

When you are writing, assume your reader knows little or nothing. Although it may seem excessive at times, it is always best to spell out everything clearly. Your reader will thank you for it! If in doubt, show your writing to a friend, colleague, or your supervisor.

2.2 The three main parts of a writing project

Almost any piece of academic writing should consist of three main parts, the introduction, the body, and the summary and conclusion. These are sometimes referred to simply as the beginning, the middle and the end. Each of these parts is discussed in detail here.

2.2.1 Writing an introduction

It is useful to remember that while a course assignment may contain a single introduction, a research report may contain within its pages a number of introductions for different sections of the work, in addition to the obligatory introductory chapter at the beginning of the report. However, although introductory chapters to dissertations and theses require a particular approach (discussed later in this guide), it is nevertheless true that all introductions have certain features in common.

2.2.1.1 The thesis statement

The most important function of an introduction is to signal to the reader what it is you are intending to discuss in your writing. This 'statement of intent' is often referred to as the *thesis statement*.

Although the thesis statement may appear at any point in your introduction, it tends to appear most frequently either at the beginning or towards the end. In this respect it is similar to a topic sentence in a paragraph (see below). An advantage of placing the thesis statement towards the end is that its relevance will be immediately clear to the reader, thanks to the contextualization provided by those sentences that precede it. If, on the other hand, your thesis statement is placed at the beginning of your introduction, then its full relevance is gradually revealed to the reader as he or she reads the sentences that follow and contextualize it. Both approaches are correct, but they each have a different effect on the reader.

Look at the following thesis statement (underlined). Here it is placed at the end of the introduction.

Example

The world today is 'smaller' than at any time in mankind's history. Cultures, lifestyles and languages mix as never before and increasingly there is emerging from this interaction what might be termed a 'global culture'. Wherever one travels, from the great metropolis to the humblest village, one cannot help but be struck by the extent to which we now share a common culture – from the clothes and designer perfumes we wear, to the films we watch, the heroes we worship and even the foods we eat. This essay will consider those factors which together have brought about this situation, and in particular the roles of the jet aeroplane, the internet and the media.

In the following example, the thesis statement is placed at the beginning of the introduction.

Example

This essay investigates the reasons underlying increased concern among consumers, particularly in the western world, over diet, the use of additives in food production and the origins of foodstuffs. In recent years scientists have raised questions about possible links between the food we eat and the increasing incidence of various types of cancer. This concern has been reflected in political discourse and the huge volume of publicity in general the issue has provoked. Not surprisingly, controversy is widespread and feelings run high among both those who defend current practices in food manufacturing and those who feel a careful critical evaluation and radical overhaul of manufacturing processes is long overdue.

TASK 1

Look at the following information. Use this information to write two introductions to an essay focusing on the implications of globalization for businesses looking to market their products around the world. In the first introduction put the thesis statement at the start; in the second introduction put it at the end. Reword the information and add to it if you wish.

Note: *The information below does not include a thesis statement. You will have to create this yourself.*

Today's world is a so-called 'Global Village'.
   Causes:

- affordable air travel;
- growth of communications industry;
- dissolution of many social and economic barriers through political activity (e.g. EU);
- demographic changes resulting from more relaxed immigration laws and improved transportation.

People of diverse cities (e.g. Sydney, Bombay, Puerto Rico, Reykjavik, Moscow, Tokyo, Johannesburg, Toronto) follow the same trends and fashions:

- the clothes they wear;
- the brands they use;
- the TV shows they watch;
- the heroes they look up to;
- the music they listen to;
- even the slang they speak.

2.2.1.2 Providing a context for your discussion

Your introduction must attempt to anchor the subject of your writing to some reference point or other that can serve as a stepping-off point for your discussion. This reference point will most likely be an idea or issue that you have come across in your reading, although it may simply be an observation based on your personal experience. What is important, though, is that by relating or linking your discussion to a reference point you are showing why it is important and relevant. You are giving your reader a reason to read your work by locating its subject matter within a broader context that they will probably be familiar with or at least interested in.

Framing or contextualizing your subject in this way also helps to draw the reader gently into your discussion. One of the most common failings of students' introductions is that they contain a thesis statement (and sometimes an indication of organization) but little or no contextualization. Although this is not strictly incorrect, it is not desirable either as it does not give the reader a chance to 'warm' to the topic. In other words, it is not very reader-friendly. Making your writing reader-friendly is important because it makes the reader more sympathetic to what you have to say.

In the following example, the information in the first paragraph provides the context for the second paragraph.

Example

For as long as there have been communities of people who share a common history and lifestyle there have been myths and legends. Most anthropologists and sociologists believe that one of the primary reasons why this is so, and why, in fact, many cultures otherwise very diverse share often remarkably similar such stories, is the need they feel to explain the world around them; a world that is often cruel, unpredictable and mysterious. Often, as time passes, these stories become so ingrained in the culture and the psyche of its people that the boundary between truth and fiction – between what actually happened or did not happen, and what is said to have happened – blurs considerably. Truth, ironically, becomes a casualty of man's need to understand and his wish to glorify his culture, create heroes and heroines etc.

The figures of Robin Hood, the stories of Adam and Eve and Camelot, and the lost world of Atlantis typify the way in which myths and legends are created and how, in the fullness of time, they take on a life of their own. It is with an analysis of these four stories, therefore, that this study of myth and legend will begin.

2.2.1.3 Indicating your organization and approach

An introduction may well include some indication of the way in which your discussion is organized and the order in which you will deal with different elements of that discussion. It may also provide a brief description of your approach to the subject matter; in other words, how you are intending to deal with the subject, the nature of your analysis and perhaps what you hope to achieve by it.

Example

> The discussion will begin with a look at the different causes of population migration and then go on to consider the social, economic and political implications, both positive and negative, of such migration. Finally, a number of suggestions will be made concerning how population migration might be more effectively controlled, followed by a review of the main points discussed and a conclusion.

Students often mistakenly believe that an introduction contains only a single paragraph. Although this is sometimes true, particularly for short course assignments, it is equally true that there is no limit to the number of paragraphs an introduction may contain. You may introduce a number of new ideas or topic changes in a single introduction, and as we shall see in our section on paragraphs, this will mean starting a new paragraph on each occasion. The rules governing when you should or should not begin a new paragraph apply in the case of introductions in just the same way as they do elsewhere in your writing.

2.2.1.4 When should I write my introduction?

Often, the best time to write an introduction is when you have otherwise finished your assignment, dissertation or thesis. This is particularly true for longer pieces of written work and/or research-based work where ideas may change during the writing-up phase. Once you have finished your writing, you may well have a better perspective on the whole work and therefore be better placed to construct a more relevant and appropriate introduction; one which better reflects the content that follows it and connects up more tidily with the conclusion.

2.2.2 Organizing the body of your writing

2.2.2.1 Paragraphs and topic sentences

Once we move beyond sentence-level, the basic unit of writing becomes the paragraph. The paragraph is a crucial and very visible unit of organization and any piece of academic writing will be certain to contain a number of paragraphs; a thesis may even contain hundreds. A paragraph is normally identifiable by its first line, which is indented slightly by about one centimetre. However, particularly in some journals, paragraphs are not always indented and instead a line is left between paragraphs to indicate where one paragraph ends and the next begins.

2.2.2.2 What is a paragraph?

A paragraph is a set of related sentences that develop one main idea. If it is a detailed or complex idea the paragraph may consist of ten or more sentences; however, if it is a simple and straightforward idea requiring little development, it may contain only one or two sentences.

2.2.2.3 When do I start a new paragraph?

You will need to begin a new paragraph whenever you introduce a new idea or shift your focus of attention. This raises the quite difficult question of how to define an idea, and this depends in part on the kind of writing you are doing. For example, if you are developing an argument, you may start a new paragraph each time you introduce a new point in that argument – although all of your points will of course need to be carefully connected if your argument is to be powerful and easily understood (see *Coherence* above). If on the other hand you are discussing a process (such as a laboratory experiment, or the phases in an evolutionary cycle), you may choose to begin a new paragraph for each stage of that process.

TASK 2

Look at the titles of the essays below. Decide how and on what basis you would organise them into paragraphs. An example has been done for you.

Example

a) *Describe and comment on China's policy for reducing its population.*

Introductory paragraph:

Realization by many LEDC governments that high birth rate = their greatest problem. It leads to shortages of resources, unemployment, crime, inadequate healthcare and schooling – and ultimately low living standards. China is a good example of this phenomenon. So how does China control its population?

Paragraph 2:

Discuss single-child policy as one of Chinese government's methods of control. Encouraged by allowing free education for single-child families, plus other allowances, priority housing + pension benefits.

Paragraph 3:

Highlight disincentives for having more than one child, for example, none of the benefits mentioned in paragraph 2 available to families with more than one child. Also the birth of additional children may invoke a fine. In the case of second or third pregnancies, women may be forced to have abortions and undergo sterilization treatment.

Paragraph 4:

Mention other rules and regulations designed to help control population, for example permission required for couples to marry and to have a child; women must be 20 and men 22 before they can marry; family planning advice and information readily available in the workplace.

Paragraph 5:

Discuss impact of these measures: By late 1990s, 230 million fewer born than if policies had not been in place. Due to their success, policies relaxed in 1999 – e.g. if only 2 children marry, they are each allowed to have 2 children; couples in rural areas allowed 2 children in order to build up the workforce.

Now try one or more of the following question titles. Your answers do not need to be as detailed as that in the example, so long as there is a clear rationale to your paragraph structure:

b) *Assess the advantages and disadvantages of transporting goods by rail as opposed to road.*
c) *What are the obstacles to free trade with the Third World and how, in your view, might they be overcome?*
d) *What is globalization and what have been some of its main causes and consequences?*
e) *Why has desertification become a problem and how might land management help address it?*
f) *Discuss the idea that despite many societies becoming more secular in recent decades, religion is currently playing as great a role in world politics as at any time in modern history.*

It is important to realize that it is not always obvious where one idea ends and a new idea begins. As a result, two different people may organize exactly the same piece of writing into slightly different paragraphs. This means that although, as we have seen, there is a general rule that ought to guide your decisions, there is often no absolutely correct way to organize your paragraphs.

2.2.2.4 The topic sentence

Each paragraph should contain a topic sentence that indicates the main subject of that paragraph, its main idea, focus or point of interest. The topic sentence usually appears at the beginning or the end of the paragraph. If it appears at the beginning, it provides a framework within which what follows is to be understood. If it appears at the end it builds a sense of expectation or anticipation in the reader as they approach it. It then confirms (or perhaps disconfirms) their expectation and in effect summarizes or makes clear the significance of the information that precedes it in the paragraph. In other words, in both cases the topic sentence serves the same purpose but in each case has a slightly different effect on the reader.

TASK 3

Look at the following paragraphs. Underline the topic sentence in each paragraph. Notice the effect on the reader of the position of the topic sentence.

---

a) *Leaves on the line are one of the main problems faced by rail operators during the autumn months. As the weather becomes colder, the trees begin shedding their leaves. Many end up on railway tracks and create a slippery surface on the lines. This can severely reduce traction and consequently slow down trains considerably. The total number of working hours lost each year as a result of this problem continues to run into many thousands, despite measures to alleviate the situation.*

b) *While the continent of Africa suffers all too often from lack of rainfall and consequent famine, Asia has to face the regular threat of typhoons, rainy seasons, earthquakes and volcanic eruptions, and America tornadoes, hurricanes, earthquakes, floods, volcanic eruptions and even extremes of temperature. By comparison, therefore, and despite occasional flash floods and relatively minor earthquakes, Europe – and the British Isles in particular – is fortunate indeed in that it rarely suffers from such catastrophic natural events.*

c) *Despite its obvious economic benefits, there still exist major concerns about the safety of genetically modified foods. This is evident in the recent spate of publicity surrounding the production of such foods as well as the growing number of lobby groups calling for their ban. What appears to concern the majority of those opposed to GM foods is the lack of scientific data on the long-term effects on the human body of consuming these foods. Yet their presence is evident in much of what we buy from supermarket shelves every day.*

d) *Day after day, animal rights protesters hampered progress on the new animal research laboratory. They blocked roads in order to prevent trucks from delivering building materials, they lobbied interest groups in Parliament, and they sabotaged each stage of its development, even resorting to arson in some cases. Perhaps most crucially, they physically threatened supporters of the laboratory and their families and thus made the potential cost of providing security for the site and its staff prohibitive. As a result, and in consultation with the government, the university abandoned its plans to build the facility.*

2.2.2.5 Main and supporting ideas

Every paragraph has one main idea (expressed in its topic sentence) and a number of supporting ideas. These supporting ideas provide a more detailed explanation of or comment on the main idea and will frequently include examples. This arrangement can be represented by Figure 2.2 (facing), which describes the structure of a piece of writing containing three paragraphs. Notice how, as you move further right in the diagram, the level of detail or specificity becomes greater.

 Supporting ideas are particularly important in academic writing. Here, statements expressing ideas are considered worthless unless there is some kind of rationale or explanation offered for them by the writer. Examples are particularly valued because they can provide concrete evidence for any claims made in the topic sentence.

TASK 4

Look at the following two paragraphs. Complete the frameworks that follow them with the paragraphs' main ideas, supporting details and (where necessary) examples.

Text A

The British and French governments agreed in January 1986 to accept a scheme which involved building two rail tunnels. Each would have a diameter of 7.3 metres, linked by a central service tunnel, with a diameter of 4.5 metres bored in advance to overcome geological problems. The

MAIN IDEA 1
    Supporting idea 1
        Example
    Supporting idea 2
    Supporting idea 3
        Example 1
        Example 2

MAIN IDEA 2
    Supporting idea 1
    Supporting idea 2
        Example

MAIN IDEA 3
    Supporting idea 1
        Example 1
        Example 2
    Supporting idea 2
    Supporting idea 3
        Example
    Supporting idea 4
        Example

FIGURE 2.2 The structure of a piece of writing.

tunnels were to connect Cheriton (England) and Frethun (France). Of the 50km of tunnel, 37km would be underwater. Although early hopes were for the first shuttle trains to be running by mid-1991, many expected even 1993 to be an optimistic date. This scheme had political advantages in that it had relatively low costs, was paid for by private investors, would have comparatively few technological risks, and could provide as many as 5000 British jobs on the tunnel construction and another 25,000 in associated industries such as concrete tunnel linings and tunnel boring equipment. It was unclear at the time which high-speed train would be used. Would it be France's TGV (Train à Grande Vitesse) or Britain's new Electra?

(Adapted from Waugh 1987)

I. _____

    1. _____

    2. ___*Linked by 4.5m-diameter service tunnel* _____

    3. _____

    4. _____

II.   ___*Hopes that trains running by mid-1991* _____

III. _____

    1. _____

    2. _____

    3. _____

    4. _____

    5. _____

        a. _____

        b. ___*tunnel boring equipment* _____

IV. _____

    1. _____

Text B

Citizens of the ten new EU members can count on major changes as their countries adjust to life in the 25-nation bloc. First, their businesses will gain easy access to a vast marketplace stretching from the Mediterranean to the Arctic. The result? No longer will it take a mountain of paperwork and a whole day at customs to process goods coming in or going out of new member countries. As more goods circulate, consumers should get a wider selection and cheaper prices. A greater range of ethnic foods, for instance, will gradually find their way onto supermarket shelves at affordable prices. Eventually workers will move as freely as the goods they produce, seeking jobs in any member country. But joining the EU has come at a cost. The new members each had to adopt 80,000 pages of new regulations and must now contribute to the Union's coffers. Initially most of the new members will receive more funds than they pay out: the EU has pledged to spend 28 billion dollars over the next three years to improve their infrastructure. Beyond economics, there is also the psychological benefit of EU membership drawing a clean line between the past and future of new member states.

I. _____

    1. ___ *Their businesses gain easy access to vast marketplace* → *less time to process*
    incoming and outgoing goods of new member countries _____

    2. _____

        a. _____

    3. _____

II. ___ *Joining the EU has come at a cost* _____

    1. _____

    2. _____

    3. _____

    4. _____

III. _____

2.2.3 The summary and conclusion

2.2.3.1 Writing a summary

<u>What is a summary?</u>

A summary is a brief restatement of the main points of your section, chapter, essay and so on. Its purpose it to remind the reader of what has been discussed. This is important because a reader can often lose track of your main points and therefore lose perspective, especially when they have been reading a lengthy or complex description or argument. A summary also helps to make clear the connection between what you have already said and what you are about to say. In other words, it helps to build links or bridges between different parts of your writing and in doing so makes it more coherent and therefore more easily understood.

<u>Where should I include a summary?</u>

If you are writing a short research assignment (2000–5000 words), it may be that you only need to write a single summary. If so, this will typically appear at the end of your essay immediately before the conclusion. If, on the other hand, you are writing a longer assignment (5000–10,000) it is more likely that you will require more than one summary; one before the conclusion, and possibly one or two others earlier on. If you are writing a research report, it is generally expected that you will include a summary at the end of each chapter.

Although any piece of academic writing should include a summary immediately prior to the main conclusion, the only other rule governing summaries is that, as a writer, you should include them only when you judge them to be necessary; do not overuse them. Only you can decide when a summary will be helpful to the reader. If you feel the amount or complexity of information may interfere with the reader's comprehension, you may need to introduce a summary to add clarity. In a research report, the amount and complexity of information can be considerable, and it is therefore quite common to find summaries not only at the end of each chapter but also at the end of many of the main sections within each chapter.

 Although a summary may appear as a separate section in an essay or research report, preceding your concluding section, it may also be incorporated into the initial part of the conclusion itself.

How do I write a good summary?

If you are intending to write a summary, you first need to introduce it. The following commonly used expressions can help you to do this:

In summary, then, the argument is as follows . . .
We might summarise the main points thus: . . .
The key points discussed so far are (as follows): . . .
This chapter has looked at a number of theories on social change. First, . . .
Three main ideas have been presented in this chapter: we began by looking at . . .

You will also need to decide the format you are going to use to present your summary. Generally, writers will opt for one of two approaches; they will either paraphrase the ideas in a condensed form, but in full prose, or they will re-present them as a bulleted or numbered list for quick and easy reference. Whichever approach you adopt, it is of course crucial that the result is considerably shorter than the original.

 Be very careful that in trying to condense information you do not distort it. A slight change of wording can sometimes have a major impact on meaning.

In the following example the same information is summarized, first in full prose, and then as a bulleted list.

Example

> This chapter has looked at a number of advantages associated with the out-of-town suburban location of offices. In particular, it identified lower rates and rental costs, a reduction typically in the level of surrounding congestion, and the fact that such offices tend to be within relatively easy reach of motorways. Furthermore, the observation was made not only that being located in the suburbs presents more in the way of opportunity for expansion, car parks etc., but that it also provides for easier access on the part of staff who, being mainly professional, managerial and skilled, will live in local, expensive suburban estates or commuter villages. Finally, it was noted that working in the suburbs generally means working in a more pleasant, healthier and less stressful environment.
>
> This chapter has identified a number of advantages associated with the out-of-town suburban location of offices. These have been shown to include:
>
> - Lower rates and rent.
> - Less traffic congestion surrounding the offices.
> - Nearer to motorways.
> - Room for expansion and car parks.
> - Easier access for staff who, being mainly professional, managerial and skilled, will live in local, expensive suburban estates or commuter villages.
> - Working in a more pleasant, healthier and less stressful environment.
>
> (Adapted from Waugh 1987)

Here is another example of an end-of-chapter summary. In this case from a PhD thesis rather than a book:

Example

> It can be seen then, that hydrological models can be classified according to the special and temporal scale for which they are used, and the extent to which they are empirically, conceptually or physically based. For this study, a three-layer conceptual 'tank-model' (consisting of both empirical and physically based sub-models), was designed to predict water table response to long-term climate change scenarios. A three-dimensional version of the same model (but with a lateral flow component) was then used to compare slope stability under different vegetation cover. The rationale for using more than one type of model stems from the view that often the best overall solution to complex multi-faceted problems may be found using a range of

different methodologies. In addition, these models proved to be more robust and consistent than equivalent physically based models.

TASK 5

Using the previous list of summary words and phrases (or any other suitable words and phrases), write a summary of an article or chapter of a book. Make sure you include only the key information. Try writing your summary first as a list of bullet points and then as full prose.

2.2.3.2 Writing a conclusion

In many ways your conclusion is the most important part of your writing, regardless of whether it is a long or short report or assignment. It is important, therefore, that you make the best possible job of it.

A good way of explaining a conclusion is by contrasting it with a summary. Students often confuse summaries and conclusions; however, the two are quite different. As we have seen, a summary simply restates, in condensed form, key information presented in the body of your writing. A conclusion, on the other hand, considers that information and then comments on it. In doing so, it makes original statements *in light of* the information presented earlier in the assignment, chapter, or entire research report. In the case of an assignment or research report, these original statements should link back to the title or thesis statement of the essay/report and address the original question or issue. In doing so, the conclusion effectively brings everything full circle and ties up all the loose ends. In the case of a chapter (of a book, research report etc.) the conclusion will comment on the subject or focal point of that particular chapter in light of what has been discussed about it.

Conclusions are therefore important because they show the relevance and significance of the information presented in the body of your writing; they are the point at which everything you have said comes together and is somehow reconciled.

Example

This chapter has been concerned with what could be said about monopoly and competition on the basis of positive economic theory. What is evident is that on many crucial points there exists no accepted theory at all, and, on other points, existing theory has been inadequately tested. It would seem that it is necessary to keep an open mind on the subject and to admit that, on the basis of existing theory, it is impossible to make out an overwhelming case either for or against monopoly as compared with competition. What is clearly needed is documentary, objective evidence, and on these grounds a great deal remains to be discovered, even at a most elementary level, about the comparison of the effects of monopoly with those of competition.

(Adapted from Lipsey 1975)

The above example is the conclusion of a chapter of a book. Our next, rather longer example (below) is the conclusion of a chapter of a PhD thesis. Notice how the final two paragraphs prepare the reader for what is to come in the following chapter(s).

Example

Conclusion

As we can see, it is only when the attitude of irony is consciously recognised – as a result of being 'foregrounded' – that the reader can argue that Huckleberry Finn attacks rather than endorses racist actions and attitudes. Our examination of the novel has allowed us to test both the echoic theory of irony and its application to a new type of case. Furthermore, I have argued for a particular interpretation of the novel based on the irony I perceive in it, and supported my claims by appeal to relevance theory in general, and the echoic account of irony in particular.

We can see then that relevance theory may have wider applications than might have first appeared to be the case. I have criticized the concept of 'foregrounding' and redefined it, and applied a relevance-theoretic approach to two common and important literary strategies traditionally analysed in terms of it, repetition and irony. They are not so unrelated as the traditional definitions suggest; in fact, by treating irony as a variety of echoic utterance we may even see a point of contact between them. Where in repetition matching forms are picked up by the language faculty, in irony an interpretive resemblance is picked up inferentially in the process of interpretation.

I have also tried to show that 'foregrounding' only occurs when the writer intends the effort required to process the 'foregrounded' elements to result in some set of intended effects. I have argued that we would be better to think of foregrounding as a description of an impression received when the writer has intentionally made an element of the text salient so that the reader will achieve extra effects for the extended effort required to process it. On this basis I distinguished between 'foregrounded' repetition and incidental or accidental repetition; I also looked at a variety of cases and showed that while we might call each one 'foregrounded', the effects differed from case to case.

We can account for the presence and effects of 'foregrounding' in terms of salience and intentionality in a relevance-theoretic framework. In fact, it is on this basis that I argued against the view that the humour and irony in Huckleberry Finn were accidental or incidental. If that were the case, then the effects could not properly be called ironic; it is not clear that we can talk of incidental or accidental irony, as we talk of incidental or accidental repetitión, say. Accidental mockery does not make much sense.

But there are still other implications resulting from applying relevance theory to literature and literary interpretations. Rather than being just another theory of reading, or even of communication, it can add substantially to long-standing literary debates and help clarify important literary issues.

It is to this application of relevance theory that I want now to turn. In the next chapter I will first look in more detail at the distinction between kinds of interpretation that I touched on briefly in this chapter. I will then propose two broad categories of interpretation. These categories are not new: in fact, they are quite traditional; but they haven't been distinguished in a consistent and principled way before. The arguments will lead inevitably to consideration of some fundamental issues in literature. Specifically, I want to see what relevance theory can add to our understanding of literariness (and not just literary interpretations). I want to see if it clarifies the characteristics of a classic. And I will examine what contributions the application of relevance theory to these two issues can make to arguments about the canon.

These are broad theoretical and literary issues, and I hardly propose to settle them here. But I do want to show that relevance theory may have some-thing of importance to add to these debates, though it may not resolve them.

 Remember, it is quite common for writers to incorporate a summary within a conclusion instead of having two separate sections.

TASK 6

Look at the two sample conclusions above. Try to distinguish summary information from the kind of new information associated with conclusions. Place any summary information in square brackets and underline any new information.

Some words and phrases commonly found in conclusions include:

In conclusion, . . .
The evidence presented indicates/suggests that . . .
Based on the evidence available, . . .
To return to our original question, it would appear that . . .
Where does this leave us in our search for an answer to our original question?
What is clear, then, is that . . .
What emerges from this discussion is . . .

There is strong evidence, to suggest that . . .
We can conclude from the foregoing discussion that . . .

Remember though, conclusions are frequently not signalled by such explicit markers as these, yet it will usually be perfectly clear that the writer is presenting their conclusions.

 TASK KEY

TASK 1 (Possible answers)

Today we live in a global world – the so-called 'global village'. Affordable air travel, the growth of the communications industry, the dissolution of many social and economic barriers through political activity and international bodies, such as the EU, and the demographic changes that have resulted from more relaxed immigration laws and improved transportation have all contributed to the emergence of this new world. In cities as diverse as Sydney, Bombay, Puerto Rico, Reykjavik, Moscow, Tokyo, Johannesburg and Toronto we see the idea of the global village manifested in the trends and fashions people follow: the clothes they wear, the brands they use, the television shows they watch, the heroes they look up to, the music they listen to, even the slang they speak. In a word, cultures are converging and becoming increasingly homogeneous. For businesses looking to market their products globally these changes are highly significant and provide unprecedented opportunities to break into new markets. This essay will look at the effects these changes have had on the marketing strategies of such businesses and the need, in particular, for increased intercultural awareness on the part of overseas marketing teams.

This essay will look at the effects the emergence of the so-called 'global village' has had on businesses looking to market their products around the world, and in particular on the need for greater intercultural awareness on the part of their marketing teams. Such businesses find themselves facing unprecedented opportunities and an accompanying need to re-evaluate their marketing strategies as a result of the emergence of this new, more connected world.

The global village has arisen as the result of affordable air travel, the growth of the communications industry, the dissolution of many social and economic barriers through political activity and international bodies, such as the EU, and the demographic changes that have resulted from more relaxed immigration laws and improved transportation. Today, in cities as diverse as Sydney, Bombay, Puerto Rico, Reykjavik, Moscow, Tokyo, Johannesburg and Toronto we see the idea of the global village manifested in the trends and fashions people follow: the clothes they wear, the brands they use, the television shows they watch, the heroes they look up to, the music they listen to, even the slang they speak. In a word, cultures are converging and becoming increasingly homogeneous.

TASK 3

a) <u>Leaves on the line are one of the main problems faced by rail operators during the autumn months.</u> As the weather becomes colder, the trees begin shedding their leaves. Many end up on railway tracks and create a slippery surface on the lines. This can severely reduce traction and consequently slow down trains considerably. The total number of working hours lost each year as a result of this problem continues to run into many thousands, despite measures to alleviate the situation.

b) While the continent of Africa suffers all too often from lack of rainfall and consequent famine, Asia has to face the regular threat of typhoons, rainy seasons, earthquakes and volcanic eruptions, and America tornadoes, hurricanes, earthquakes, floods, volcanic eruptions and even extremes of temperature. By comparison, therefore, and despite occasional flash floods and relatively minor earthquakes, Europe – and <u>the British Isles in particular – is fortunate indeed in that it rarely suffers from such catastrophic natural events.</u>

c) <u>Despite its obvious economic benefits, there still exist major concerns about the safety of genetically modified foods.</u> This is evident in the recent spate of publicity surrounding the production of such foods as well as the growing number of lobby groups calling for their ban. What appears to concern the majority of those opposed to GM foods is the lack of scientific data on the long-term effects on the human body of consuming these foods. Yet their presence is evident in much of what we buy from supermarket shelves every day.

d) Day after day, animal rights protesters hampered progress on the new animal research laboratory. They blocked roads in order to prevent trucks from delivering building materials, they lobbied interest groups in Parliament, and they sabotaged each stage of its development, even resorting to arson in some cases. Perhaps most crucially, they physically threatened supporters of the laboratory and their families and thus made the potential cost of providing security for the site and its staff prohibitive. <u>As a result, and in consultation with the government, the university abandoned its plans to build the facility.</u>

TASK 4

Text A

I. Jan '86 B & F agreed to build 2 rail tunnels
    1. Each a diameter of 7.3m
    2. Linked by 4.5m-diameter service tunnel

       3. To connect Cheriton & Frethun
       4. 37km of tunnel underwater
II.   Hopes that trains running by mid-1991
III. Scheme had political advantages
       1. Low costs
       2. Paid for by private investors
       3. Few technological risks
       4. Up to 5000 construction jobs
       5. 25000 jobs in associated industries
          a. concrete tunnel linings
          b. tunnel boring equipment
IV. Unclear which train would be used
       1. TGV vs Electra

Text B

I.   Major changes for new EU member states
       1. Their businesses gain easy access to vast marketplace → less time to process incoming and outgoing goods of new member countries
       2. Consumers get a wider selection and cheaper prices – e.g. ethnic foods on supermarket shelves at affordable prices
       3. Workers will move more freely, seeking jobs in any member country
II.   Joining the EU has come at a cost
       1. Each new member has had to adopt 80.000 pages of new regulations
       2. New members must contribute to the Union's coffers
       3. Initially most new states will receive more funds than they pay out
       4. EU has pledged 28 billion dollars over next 3 years to improve their infrastructure
III. New member states benefit psychologically from drawing a clean line between their past and future

TASK 6

[This chapter has been concerned with what could be said about monopoly and competition on the basis of positive economic theory. What is evident is that on many crucial points there exists no accepted theory at all, and, on other points, existing theory has been inadequately tested.] It would seem that it is necessary to keep an open mind on the subject and to admit that, on the basis of existing theory, it is impossible to make out an overwhelming case either for or against monopoly as compared with competition. What is clearly needed is documentary, objective evidence, and on these grounds a great deal remains to be discovered, even at a most elementary level, about the comparison of the effects of monopoly with those of competition.

Conclusion

[As we can see, it is only when the attitude of irony is consciously recognized – as a result of being 'foregrounded' – that the reader can argue that Huckleberry Finn attacks rather than endorses racist actions and attitudes. Our examination of the novel has allowed us to test both the echoic theory of irony and its application to a new type of case. Furthermore, I have argued for a particular interpretation of the novel based on the irony I perceive in it, and supporting my claims by appeal to relevance theory in general, and the echoic account of irony in particular.]

We can see then that relevance theory may have wider applications than might have first appeared to be the case. [I have criticized the concept of 'foregrounding' and redefined it, and applied a relevance-theoretic approach to two common and important literary strategies traditionally analysed in terms of it, repetition and irony.] They are not so unrelated as the traditional definitions suggest; in fact, by treating irony as a variety of echoic utterance we may even see a point of contact between them. Where in repetition matching forms are picked up by the language faculty, in irony an interpretive resemblance is picked up inferentially in the process of interpretation.

[I have also tried to show that 'foregrounding' only occurs when the writer intends the effort required to process the 'foregrounded' elements to result in some set of intended effects. I have argued that we would be better to think of foregrounding as a description of an impression received when the writer has intentionally made an element of the text salient so that the reader will achieve extra effects for the extended effort required to process it. On this basis I distinguish between 'foregrounded' repetition and incidental or accidental repetition. I also looked at a variety of cases and showed that while we might call each one 'foregrounded', the effects differed from case to case.]

We can account for the presence and effects of 'foregrounding' in terms of salience and intentionality in a relevance-theoretic framework. In fact, it is on this basis that I argued against the view that the humour and irony in Huckleberry Finn were accidental or incidental. If that were the case, then the effects could not properly be called ironic; it is not clear that we can talk of incidental or accidental irony, as we talk of incidental or accidental repetition, say. Accidental mockery does not make much sense.

But there are still other implications resulting from applying relevance theory to literature and literary interpretations. Rather than being just another theory of reading, or even of communication, it can add substantially to long-standing literary debates and help clarify important literary issues.

It is to this application of relevance theory that I want now to turn. In the next chapter I will first look in more detail at the distinction between kinds of interpretation that I touched on briefly in this chapter. I will then propose two broad categories of interpretation. These categories are not new: in fact, they are quite traditional but they haven't been distinguished in a consistent and principled way before. The arguments will lead inevitably to consideration of some fundamental issues in literature. Specifically, I want to see what relevance theory can add to our understanding of literariness (and not just literary interpretations). I want to see if it clarifies the characteristics of a classic. And I will examine what contributions the application of relevance theory to these two issues can make to arguments about the canon.

These are broad theoretical and literary issues, and I hardly propose to settle them here. But I do want to show that relevance theory may have something of importance to add to these debates, though it may not resolve them.

2.3 Citation, referencing and paraphrasing

Referring to the ideas of other scholars and established writers in your work is important because it makes your writing more potent and convincing by showing your knowledge of the subject area (see also Sections 4.4 and 6.7). You should quote other scholars in your field (and sometimes in other fields) in order to contextualize your ideas and support the claims you make. A note of caution though: do not over-quote; most of the work you produce must be your own and not a string of quotations from other people's work!

Before looking at how to quote sources properly, let's briefly look at one of the biggest dangers that faces budding academics: *plagiarism* – a word that is being mentioned increasingly frequently these days, particularly since the proliferation of material now so readily available on the internet.

2.3.1 Plagiarism: what is it and how can I avoid it?

Citing means acknowledging clearly the sources of any ideas you use in your writing which are not your own. *Plagiarism* is when writers fail to do this. The penalties for plagiarism can be very severe, including failing a paper or examination; indeed, there is usually a warning against plagiarism included on assignment sheets and in examination regulations. Furthermore, it is increasingly common for students to have to submit, along with their assignments, a signed statement to the effect that they are aware of the penalties for plagiarism and that the work they are submitting is their own except where reference to other sources is explicitly made. If you fail to cite your sources, it is assumed you are implicitly claiming that the ideas expressed are your own; it is therefore considered dishonest and intentionally misleading if the marker or examiner finds instead that the ideas belong to someone else. In the following pages, we will address the question of how to cite sources correctly and therefore avoid any accusations of plagiarism while simultaneously enriching the quality and credibility of your work.

2.3.2 In-text referencing

Citations, then, are a crucial part of academic writing and appear at points in your text where reference is made to others' work – called *in-text referencing*. They refer the reader to the reference list placed at the end of your own work and normally referred to as the Bibliography – something we shall visit in Section 6.12.

2.3.2.1 Different referencing systems

There are a number of different referencing styles used in academic writing and you should consult your department, tutor or supervisor to find out which style *you* should use, as this can vary according to institution and academic discipline. Whatever the style, though, it is important that you are consistent in your application of it. The style most commonly used, particularly in the Humanities and Social Science disciplines is the Harvard referencing system, also sometimes referred to as the 'author–date' system. Here, the author's name and the date of publication of cited works are given in the body of the text, and the bibliography is listed alphabetically by author. It is this system that we shall focus on here and which is used in all the examples that follow.

The other widely used style is known as the Vancouver referencing system, also called the 'author–number' system. This system tends to be adopted more within the science disciplines and differs from the Harvard system in that it uses a number series to indicate references in the body of the text. These references are then listed in the bibliography in the same numerical order as they appear in the text. The main advantage of the Vancouver style is that the main text reads more easily or fluently without the citations 'getting in the way of' the meaning by breaking up the text. In addition, because references in the bibliography are directly correlated to numbers, the reader spends less time searching alphabetically for the first author of a reference. An in-text reference formatted according to the Vancouver style might appear as follows:

> Although many very prominent scientists believe that such procedures raise serious ethical issues, others, most notably Adams (2,3) and McCormack (4), argue that such issues are exaggerated and anyway should play second fiddle to the potentially enormous health benefits.

Although the Harvard and Vancouver systems are generally cited as the two main systems, there are numerous others and this can be a source of confusion, particularly as within each of them there can be minor variations. Although your first port of call should always be your supervisor/department, we have included in the Appendix a series of links according to discipline and the particular styles associated with each. For more information on these systems you might find the following books and website helpful:

- *The Complete Guide to Referencing and Avoiding Plagiarism* by Colin Neville, 2007.
- *Harvard Style: Style Manual for Authors, Editors and Printers* (6th edn), 2002.
- *The Oxford Guide to Style* by Robert Ritter, 2002.
- http://www.citethemright.co.uk/index.html

Whichever referencing system you use, in order to ensure that you have the information you need for accurate referencing later on, whenever you make notes you should detail the source of those notes as follows:

- the author's full name(s);
- the title of the publication;
- the title of the article (if a journal);
- the date of publication;
- the publisher (if a book);
- the page numbers (required for direct quotations or journal articles);
- the volume number (if a journal).

You will need to use some of this information for in-text citations and all of it when you come to write your bibliography. Make sure you record this information as you take notes, for it can be very difficult and time consuming to try and do this at a later date when you may find that you have forgotten where you sourced your information. Bear in mind that bibliographic management software packages (see Section 6.12) will only work if there is a database containing complete records of all your references. Without such records this convenient, time-saving software cannot do its job – which means that you will have to pay somebody else to do it, or do it yourself. The point: a little forethought can save you time, money and considerable frustration!

There are two occasions when you will need to cite references within your text:

1. When you directly quote an original source.
2. When you use information or ideas taken from another source which you express in your own words (paraphrasing).

Let's now look at these two cases in more detail.

2.3.3 Quoting primary and secondary sources

Quoting a primary source means quoting *directly* a writer's own ideas precisely as they appear in the original work where they were published. In contrast, quoting a secondary source means quoting a writer who has expressed the ideas of the original writer in his or her own words, and in doing so has interpreted and paraphrased (see below) the original writer. In other words, what *you* end up writing is two steps removed from the original source. When you are reading a secondary source, you are not reading the actual words of the original author of those ideas but a 'second-hand' version, which may not necessarily reflect fairly and accurately the original text. As such, wherever possible, it is preferable to quote primary sources. If you do wish to quote a secondary source, be sure to read the primary source on which it is based; that way you can be certain you are not misrepresenting the ideas of other scholars. Equally, you should never cite an article based only on an abstract – also a type of secondary source; always read the article in full.

2.3.3.1 Quoting directly: shorter stretches of text

Quoting directly means using the exact words of the original writer. There are two ways in which this can be done. If it is a short quotation of a few words, or perhaps a sentence, it can normally be included in the main body of the paragraph and must appear within single quotation marks (double quotation marks can be used for quotations within quotations). You do not need to begin a new line. Look at the following examples:

White (2001, p. 65) argues that 'even before the onset of World War I the British empire was on the wane'.

or

White argues that 'even before the onset of World War I the British Empire was on the wane' (2001, p. 65).

or

White (2001, p. 65) argues, 'even before the onset of World War I the British empire was on the wane'.

Although, according to Davies (1990, p. 106), 'it was the work of Hymes that was the main catalyst for the onset of a communicative approach to language teaching', there is good reason to believe that the seeds of the approach had been sown long before.

Notice how, in these examples, only the year and page number appear in parentheses. This is because the name occurs naturally in the sentence either before or after the quotation. In contrast, in the example below, the name does not occur naturally in the sentence outside of the quotation. It is necessary, therefore, to include it in parentheses, along with the year and page number.

It has been observed that 'Prominent among the assets of the English language must be considered the mixed character of its vocabulary' (Baugh 1968, p. 9).

Where a quotation is incorporated within a larger sentence, the full-stop comes after the reference, not between the quotation and the reference.

If you are quoting two authors, use the following form:

Brooks and Weatherston (2000) explain that . . .
Davies and Frugett (1997) argue that . . .

If you are quoting more than two authors, use the following form:

Hall et al. have suggested that . . .
Gregg et al. make a stronger claim, insisting that . . .

2.3.3.2 *Use of et al.*

'et al.', as used in the above two examples, means 'and others'. It is only used in references that appear within the main body of the text or in footnotes, and not in the bibliography, where the names of all authors should be provided.

Although, in the past, single quotation marks were preferred in British academic culture, increasingly double quotation marks are being used. These are preferred in the United States and have at least one advantage: they avoid the situation where a reader might be momentarily misled into thinking that they have come to the end of a quotation when they see an apostrophe. However, whether you choose to use double or single quotation marks, if you face a situation where you are citing a quotation within a quotation, you need to use a different type of quotation mark. Look at these examples:

The Prime Minister stated that 'describing the capital's transportation system as "hopelessly unreliable and outdated" was unfair and inaccurate'.

> The Prime Minister stated that "describing the capital's transportation system as 'hopelessly unreliable and outdated' was unfair and inaccurate".

2.3.3.3 Quoting directly: longer stretches of text

If you wish to quote a longer stretch of text, it is best to leave a line before and after the quotation and to indent it. It is also customary to use single spacing, and a slightly smaller font is also permissible. Look at this example:

Both competencies, he argued, are part of the same developmental matrix, and as such linguistic theory needs to

> ... account for the fact that a normal child acquires knowledge of sentences, not only as grammatical, but also as appropriate. He or she acquires competence as to when to speak, when not, and as to what to talk about with whom, where, when and in what manner.
>
> (Hymes 1972, p. 277)

It was this need to understand the non-grammatical aspect of the developmental matrix which motivated that area of inquiry known as the ethnography of communication.

2.3.3.4 Introducing quotations

If you are quoting longer sections of text in this way they are sometimes preceded either with a colon (as in the example below), a comma, or sometimes no punctuation at all. Look at the following quotation introduced in three different ways:

In his introduction to 'The Poverty of Historicism,' Popper states:

> Scientific interest in social and political questions is hardly less old than scientific interest in cosmology and physics; and there were periods in antiquity when the science of society might have seemed to have advanced further than the science of nature.
>
> (Popper 1957, p. 1)

Scientific interest in social and political questions is, according to Popper,

> hardly less old than scientific interest in cosmology and physics; and there were periods in antiquity when the science of society might have seemed to have advanced further than the science of nature.
>
> (Popper 1957, p. 1)

In his introduction to 'The Poverty of Historicism,' Popper states that

> Scientific interest in social and political questions is hardly less old than scientific interest in cosmology and physics; and there were periods in antiquity when the science of society might have seemed to have advanced further than the science of nature.
>
> (Popper 1957, p. 1)

There may be times when you wish to omit part of a quotation if, for example, it is not strictly relevant to your discussion. In this case, you must indicate that the quotation is not complete by using a series of dots (usually three).

Example

> Scientific interest in social and political questions is hardly less old than scientific interest in cosmology and physics; and there were periods . . . when the science of society might have seemed to have advanced further than the science of nature.
>
> (Popper 1957, p. 1)

As you will see from the above examples, there are a number of phrases that can be used to introduce a direct quotation, and they are almost always in the present tense. Here are some common ones. Notice the difference in punctuation between those in the left list and those in the right list.

X states that '. . .	*As X states, '. . .*
X argues that '. . .	*As X claims, '. . .*
X claims that '. . .	*As X suggests, '. . .*
X has suggested that '. . .	*As X proposes, '. . .*
X proposes that '. . .	*As X maintains, '. . .*
X maintains that '. . .	*According to X, '. . .*

 These phrases can also be used to introduce a paraphrase.

2.3.4 Reporting the ideas of others using paraphrase

We have looked at how to use the original words of other writers in your own writing. Paraphrasing is an alternative way of incorporating the ideas of other writers by expressing them in your *own* words, by 'reporting' them. Look at the following example. First is the original text and following it is a paraphrase of that text.

Example

Many others before Darwin had suggested that all life on earth was interrelated. Darwin's revolutionary insight was to perceive the mechanism that brought these changes about. By doing so he replaced a philosophical speculation with a detailed description of a process, supported by an abundance of evidence, that could be tested and verified; and the reality of evolution could no longer be denied.

Put briefly, his argument was this: all individuals of the same species are not identical. In one clutch of eggs from, for example, a giant tortoise, there will be some hatchlings which, because of their genetic constitution, will develop longer necks than others. In times of drought they will be able to reach leaves and so survive. Their brothers and sisters, with shorter necks, will starve and die. So those best fitted to their surroundings will be selected and be able to transmit their characteristics to their offspring. After a great number of generations, tortoises on the arid islands will have longer necks than those on the watered islands. And so one species will have given rise to another.

This concept did not become clear in Darwin's mind until long after he had left the Galapagos. For twenty-five years he painstakingly amassed evidence to support it. Not until 1859, when he was forty-eight years old, did he publish it and even then he was driven to do so only because another young naturalist, Alfred Wallace, working in Southeast Asia, had formulated the same idea. He called the book in which he set out his theory in detail, *The Origin of Species by Means of Natural Selection or the Preservation of Favoured Races in the Struggle for Life.*

Now look at this paraphrase:

Although Darwin was not alone in thinking that all life was interrelated, he went a crucial step further by providing irrefutable evidence to support the idea; evidence collected over twenty-five years. He argued that because not all individuals of the same species are identical, only those better suited to survive in their environment would live; the others would die. Those who survived would pass on their characteristics to their offspring, and after the passing of many generations a new species would arise that would automatically exhibit those characteristics and therefore be naturally suited to their environment. He finally published his findings in 1859 in a book entitled *The Origin of Species by Means of Natural Selection.*

In order to paraphrase effectively you need to do four things:

1. You need to summarize the idea you are paraphrasing.
2. You need to express the idea using your own words. A good way of doing this is to take notes as you read the original text and where possible use synonyms. Another way is to read the original text, then, when you have finished, write it from memory using your own words.
3. You need to make sure that your paraphrase flows smoothly and expresses the original idea accurately.
4. You need to acknowledge your sources just as if you were quoting them directly.

 Whether you quote directly or report using paraphrase, the way in which you cite the original author of the idea and the publication where it is located is the same in both cases. Although different publications may use slightly different conventions, the information is typically placed in parentheses in the following way:

(Taylor 1998, p. 34) or (Taylor 1998: 34)

Most of the instances of paraphrase found in academic writing are considerably shorter than the above example, as we can see if we look at the following paraphrase of an earlier quotation:

Original quotation:

'Prominent among the assets of the English language must be considered the mixed character of its vocabulary' (Baugh 1968, p. 9).

Paraphrase:

One of the most important features of the English language is the varied nature of its vocabulary (Baugh 1968).

or

According to Baugh (1968), one of the most important features of the English language is the varied nature of its vocabulary.

Introductory phrases used when paraphrasing include:

Worthington and Britton (1994) explain that . . .
Kotler et al. (2000) have suggested that . . .
. . . as observed by Midler (2006), who argues that . . .

One economist (Fischer 1972) has criticized this theory, but Hack (1984) claims it . . .
Epstein (2005) takes the view that . . .
As Privet states/notes, . . .

There may be occasions when you wish to refer simultaneously to information provided by a number of different sources. These sources should be listed in chronological order.

Example

This represents an alternative view of advertising which has been put forward by some writers (Stigler 1961, Telser 1964, Nelson 1978, Littlechild 1982), yet remained marginalized for the most part.

Sometimes you may use more than one source by the same author and with the same year of publication. In this case, the works should be listed alphabetically under the author's name in the bibliography (see Section 6.12), with a lower-case letter (starting with the letter 'a') following the year of publication. The same style is used for the in-text reference and is illustrated below:

Jones (1995a) refers to this phenomenon in terms of . . .
Jones (1995b) describes this experiment as . . .

Secondary sources should be cited as follows:

This process has been identified as having three main stages (Duckworth 2001, cited in Black 2006).

Here Duckworth is the primary source, although you have 'read' him via Black, the secondary source.

 Remember: if the ideas cited in a secondary source are crucial to your own line of argument and thus also to the credibility of your work, it is essential that you consult the original to ensure that the author of those ideas is not being misinterpreted, wilfully or otherwise.

TASK 1

Paraphrase each of the following two passages on Iraq

Between 1973 and 1979, as oil income exploded from 13.3 to 41.6 billion in today's dollars, Iraq was transformed from an agrarian to an industrial economy, and everyone, even the Shiites, benefited. Then came the Iran-Iraq war, followed by the gulf war, and the UN sanctions. Until the 1990s many regarded Shiites as the backbone of the middle class; twelve years of sanctions, however, made the middle class destitute and passive, and hindered their ability to emerge as a group that advocates political change. Many of Iraq's middle class left to live in exile, and those that remained tried to become invisible, living in half-vacant houses, having sold possessions to pay for essentials. But the truly impoverished lived in Saddam City (since renamed Sadr City), a slum in Baghdad that is home to nearly two million Shiites.

(Adapted from *National Geographic*, June 2004)

The Shiites have long dreamed of rising to power in Iraq, a dream that was first squashed when, in alliance with the Sunnis, they failed in their rebellion against the British colonial power in 1920 – a time of occupation that many older Iraqis still look back on with bitterness. To the Shiites' great disappointment, the British then installed a foreign Sunni monarch, the Hashemite King Faisal, to lead the modern state of Iraq, paving the way for decades of Sunni dominance.

Both the monarchy and later the Baath Party, which came to power in 1968, emphasised the idea of Arab unity over a distinct Iraqi identity. Though made up primarily of Sunni Arabs, the Baathists were staunchly secular. They distrusted the 'backward' and 'fanatic' Shiites, depicting them as Arab-hating Persians whose loyalties lay with Iran. Throughout the '70s the Baathists stepped up the oppression of Shiites, which fuelled the rise of al-Dawa ('the Call'), a political party dedicated to the establishment of an Islamic state in Iraq. Al-Dawa's resistance only increased the persecution. The Baathists executed five clerics without trial in 1974. Three years later, after Shiite demonstrations in the shrine cities, eight more clerics were executed and 15 were sentenced to life imprisonment.

The suppression got even worse after the Iranian revolution. Emboldened by the creation of an Islamic state next door, tens of thousands of religious Shiites joined the resistance party and began attacking Baath offices. As Al-Dawa became more militant, membership of the party became illegal, and anyone who assisted a member could be imprisoned or executed.

(Adapted from *National Geographic*, June 2004)

TASK 2

Write down six short quotations from an academic text. Then, paraphrase them citing the correct references. Try to vary where, in your paraphrases, the references appear as this will give you practice in employing some of the range of phrases typically used when introducing a paraphrase.

2.3.5 Tips for using electronic sources (see also section 4.3)

Today, the internet has become an integral and indispensable part of assignment writing and the research process – almost everybody uses it to some extent and is expected to have access to it; indeed, without such access it will soon become almost impossible to engage fully in any kind of academic study and to conduct research effectively. Increasingly, electronic references are included on course reading lists, and most Library and Information Services now provide helpful information on and links to on-line sources. However, while it is a wonderful and abundant source of information that you will certainly want to take good advantage of, the internet needs to be treated with some caution. While on-line journal articles or official websites, such as those set up by government departments, may be useful and sound sources of information – many of the former having undergone a process of peer review – commercial and private websites frequently contain unreliable and/or biased information and will therefore frequently require verification. Furthermore, electronic information may change or disappear completely. Finally, internet-based materials may be subject to copyright restrictions requiring permission for them to be reproduced elsewhere. If you do plan to use electronic sources, consider the following tips:

- Critically evaluate the sources and treat them as 'questionable until proven sound'. Be particularly sceptical if they do not cite a specific author or publication date.
- If there is no author name, try to identify the institutional body presenting the source; alternatively, email the Webmaster for advice.
- Save and print all documents you wish to cite. Sometimes web-based material suddenly disappears or is poorly archived.
- Check whether any copyright restrictions apply. If they do, make sure you secure permission to use the source material.
- Always bookmark useful websites.

Electronic sources cited within your text should be listed in the same way as printed works – the author's surname followed by the date of publication in parentheses.

Example:

> Simmons recognizes this when he states that, 'few marketing specialists pay adequate attention to the issues of differing cultural perceptions' (Simmons, 2000, www + site).

Example:

> She states that, 'without a doubt, the issue of conceptual differences between cultures has been largely ignored' (Bertorelli 2008, email communication).

When referring to a general resource, service or homepage, include the url.

Examples:

> 'Such documentation is typically found at dedicated governmental websites such as http://www.immi.gov.au'

> 'Further details of these trends can be found at the organisation's website: <http://www.tectonics.data.org/>'

> 'One such site devoted to the European Union is: http://europa.eu.int/index_en.htm'

Eventually, you will need to list in alphabetical order all those sources you have cited during the course of your discussion. This list should appear at the end of the work, in the references. For details on how to list sources in your reference section, go to Section 6.12.

2.3.6 Diagrams and illustrations

Just as the authors of ideas used in your writing need to be given due recognition through good referencing practices, so too scanned or electronic images need to be acknowledged by citation, as these are also regarded as the 'intellectual property' of their creators.

Finally, never cite a work you have not read yourself. Do not rely on abstracts or the paraphrasing and interpretation of others; obtain the original text and cite that. Avoid citing unpublished works as their credibility will always be questionable, and always check your references before finally submitting your work – during the course of your research, new editions of books you have cited may have become available, and it is important that your bibliography is as current as possible.

TASK KEY

TASK 1

Possible answers:

Between 1973 and 1979, Iraq's oil income expanded by $28.3 billion in today's dollars, transforming the country from an agrarian to an industrial economy and benefiting the population at large. However, following the Iran–Iraq war, the gulf war and 12 years of UN sanctions, the previously affluent Shiites, the backbone of the middle class, became impoverished. As a result, they lost their political influence, with many deciding to become invisible or live in exile.

In 1920 the Shiites and the Sunnis united in an unsuccessful attempt to overthrow the British colonial power. Much to the displeasure of the ambitious Shiites, the British responded by inaugurating a foreign Sunni monarch, the Hashemite King Faisal, thereby setting the stage for an era of Sunni supremacy.
   In 1968 the Baath Party came to power, and was comprised of mainly Sunni Arabs who, being strongly secular, were suspicious of the Shiites, whom they considered backward and fanatical, portraying them as Arab-hating Persians with loyalty to Iran. During the 1970s, the Baathists, who gave primacy to the idea of Arab unity rather than a distinct Iraqi identity, increased their persecution of the Shiites, leading to the rise of al-Dawa, a political party committed to the creation of an Islamic State in Iraq. This, however, only led to further persecution, including the execution of five clerics without trial in 1974, and another eight in 1977 following Shiite demonstrations three years later.
   The Iranian revolution exacerbated the situation as thousands of Shiites joined the resistance party, heartened by the formation of the Islamic state of Iran. Al-Dawa became increasingly militant, and membership of the party consequently became illegal with executions or imprisonment constituting the penalty for those who assisted any of its members.

2.4 Using footnotes

As a general rule, it is best not to use footnotes. Instead, try to include any relevant information in the main body of your text. Occasionally, however, you may wish to use footnotes. There are two main reasons for doing so:

1. You wish to provide additional information or to make a point briefly which is not directly relevant to your immediate discussion but is nevertheless related and of potential interest. Look at the following examples:

Example Main text:

> While controls on local government spending, and particularly the system of penalties associated with the Rates Bill of 1988, were found threatening by Conservative local authorities,[1] the ideal of restricting government expenditure resonated with longstanding Conservative beliefs that predated Thatcherite policies.

Footnote:

[1] Leaders of the Conservative controlled Association of County Councils regarded rate capping as a threat to local authorities' right to determine their own rates but refrained from public criticism of central government after being assured that only 'hard left' authorities were likely to be capped (Butcher et al. 1990 p. 71).

Example Main text:

> And while council house sales inevitably reduced the source of revenue available to subsidise the General Rate Fund, the dependence of the authority on this source of income reduced as the decade progressed with no recorded transfers from the Housing Revenue Account to the General Rate Fund between 1987–1988 and 1989–1990.[3]

Footnote:

[3] Fenland District's dependence on such revenues may also have fallen as a function of the changing economic structure of the district. Between 1981 and 1990, the product of a penny rate per hereditament increased from 83.4% to 86.7% of the mean average for non-metropolitan districts of England and Wales.

2. You wish to give details of a source. Nowadays, instead of using footnotes, most writers choose to include this information in their bibliography at the end of their essay, research report and so on. However, occasionally sources will be included as footnotes. This tends to happen when the source is not of direct relevance to the immediate discussion but is nevertheless relevant at some level and may be of interest to the reader. Look at these examples:

Example Main text:

> The odds ration (OR) is defined as the ration of the odds for $x = 1$ to the odds for $x = 0$.[3]

Footnote:

[3] For a more detailed explanation of the odds ratio, see Hosmer and Lemeshow (2000).

Main Text:

Without doubt, one of the most important factors in reducing the number of casualties from earthquakes is the way in which, increasingly, earthquake-resistant technology is being designed into buildings,[2] particularly those more at risk, such as skyscrapers and high-rise blocks.

Footnote:

[2] See Everest (1999) for an in-depth discussion of developments in earthquake-resistant architectural design techniques and strategies.

2.4.1 Using Latin and English words and abbreviations with quotations and footnotes

There are a number of words and abbreviations frequently used in academic writing. Being familiar with them and understanding them will not only help you in your reading but will also help you to be more efficient and economical in your writing. Here are the most important words and phrases you should know.

Latin	
cf.	compare (Also see *cp* below)
circa	about (a specified date or number – e.g. circa 1999)
et al.	and others
et seq.	and the following (pages, material, etc.)
ibid.	in the same book, article (used to refer to a book or article mentioned immediately above; e.g. *ibid.*, p. 77).
infra	below or further on in a book, article etc.
loc. cit.	in the article, chapter or section cited before. (Note: You must give the author's name.) e.g. Davies, *loc. cit.*
op. cit.	in the book cited before. (Note: You must give the author's name and a page reference; e.g. Davies, *op. cit.*, p. 107).
passim	throughout or at many points in a book, article etc. (used when a topic is referred to several times in a book, article etc. to which you are referring; e.g. Ljubec 1989, pp. 43–56, *passim*).
(sic)	thus used, spelt etc. (used when the person you are quoting has made a mistake, such as a spelling mistake, and you want to indicate to your reader(s) that it is not *your* mistake.
viz.	namely, that is to say, in other words

English

above/ *see above*	appearing earlier in the chapter, essay, article etc.
below/ *see below*	appearing later in the chapter, essay, article etc.
cp./ *compare*	compare this with another idea or what another writer says on the topic.
ed.; eds.	editor/edition; editors/editions
ff.	and the following pages; e.g. Nesbitt et al. 2001, p. 24 ff. means page 24 and the following pages of Nesbitt et al.
ms.; mss.	manuscript; manuscripts
n.d.	no date given, or no date available
n.p.	no place given
n.pub.	no publisher given
no.; nos.	number; numbers
p.; pp.	page; pages; e.g. Davies 2008, pp. 88–92.
trans.	translator/translated/translation
vol.; vols.	volume; volumes

3

What do I need to know about writing style?

3.1 Writing clearly and concisely • 3.2 Level of formality (register) •
3.3 Using gender-neutral language • 3.4 Reading other research projects

Style is one aspect of report writing that both native and non-native students often feel uncertain about. It is difficult to know exactly what makes 'good style' and even more difficult to explain. This is largely because, as native speakers, we tend to learn good style through the processes of reading and writing and never question what it is that creates or underlies it. What complicates matters further is the fact that ideas about good style change over time, and what used to be considered good style is no longer necessarily so today. In other words, it is a rather fluid, changeable concept, something of a moving target. And yet, there are certain expectations about the way in which ideas should be expressed in academic writing. Some attempt therefore needs to be made at describing the notion of 'good style', or what is considered acceptable practice.

Fortunately, there are a few general principles that can help provide you with direction in the way you express yourself when writing up your assignments or research. These can be dealt with under a few simple headings.

3.1 Writing clearly and concisely

This is a good example of the way in which ideas about good academic writing have changed. It used to be the case that long, complex sentences and sophisticated vocabulary were an indication that the writer was erudite and well educated. They were therefore viewed positively, even if they made the reader work harder! Today, however, simpler, more straightforward vocabulary and writing which allows the reader easier access to ideas is preferred.

Avoid complex and lengthy sentences. Clarity is essential, so you need to make your writing as easy to read and accessible to your reader as possible. Keep your sentences short and to the point, but not so short as to sound 'choppy' and lack flow. Be relevant, make every word count, and try not to express more than one idea in each sentence.

There are a number of techniques to consider when aiming for clarity and conciseness, but two of the most important are parallel structure and sentence combining. Let's now look at each of these in turn.

3.1.1 Parallel structure

Parallel structure refers to sentence elements that are similar (parallel) in grammatical form and therefore create a kind of balance or symmetry. These elements can be words, phrases or clauses that are joined by the coordinating conjunctions *and, but, or, for,* or by paired coordinating conjunctions such as *both . . . and, (n)either . . . (n)or, not only . . . but also.* Elements that are contrasted using *not* may also be expressed as parallel structures.

Remember:

- parallel structure should be used when dealing with more than one item in a list;
- the grammatical form chosen for the first item in a sentence should be used for subsequent items in the same sentence. In other words, it serves as a kind of model.

Examples

- Her frequent <u>absences</u> (*noun*) and poor <u>motivation</u> (*noun*) caused her to fail.
- He was fired not only <u>for his inexcusable absences</u> (*prepositional phrase*) from the office, but also <u>for his rudeness to clients</u> (*prepositional phrase*).
- Children often do <u>what they want to do</u> (*relative clause*), not <u>what they should do</u> (*relative clause*).

A lack of parallelism in a sentence can obscure meaning and be awkward to read.

Look at the following example of a longer sentence which lacks parallel structure:

This paper will discuss [1] trade policy considerations, [2] the use of trade policy in developing countries and [3] how advanced countries apply strategic trade policy.

The parallelism breaks down with item 3, which uses a different grammatical construction from items 1 and 2. Items 1 and 2 employ noun phrases while 3 begins with a relative clause. Look at the same sentence again, but with 3 transformed into a noun phrase so that it is 'parallel' with 1 and 2.

This paper will discuss [1] trade policy considerations, [2] the use of trade policy in developing countries and [3] the application of strategic trade policy in advanced countries.

Sentences of this kind (which often read as lists) are frequently found in introductions, summaries and conclusions to essays and research reports.
Sir Winston Churchill used parallel structure to great effect in what is probably his most famous speech:

We shall fight in France, we shall fight on the seas and oceans, we shall fight with growing strength and growing confidence in the air. We shall fight on the beaches, we shall fight on the landing grounds, we shall fight in the fields and in the streets, we shall fight in the hills, we shall never surrender . . .

It is the parallelism here (together with repetition) that gives this speech its potency and makes it memorable. Notice how the parallel structure exists on two levels: the repetition of the future verb tense (we shall fight) and the repetition of prepositional phrases (in France, on the seas and [on the] oceans, etc.) – the latter echo each other, sandwiched as they are between the verbs. In addition, there is the added parallelism of 'growing strength and growing confidence'. The climax of the speech is reached when the word 'fight' is replaced by 'surrender' but the echo of parallelism is still there with the continued use of 'shall'.
Parallelism is also frequently used in advertisements to reinforce the name of a product as well as its qualities. Look at this example:

Honeysilk shampoo ... so soft; Honeysilk shampoo ... so luxurious; Honeysilk shampoo ... so enriching and refreshing. With Honeysilk shampoo your hair will never look or feel the same again.

Now examine how Bertrand Russell, the mathematician and philosopher, uses parallel structure in his autobiography:

Three passions, simple but overwhelmingly strong, have governed my life: the longing for love, the search for knowledge, and unbearable pity for the suffering of mankind (*noun phrases*).

Having created a parallel framework, Russell goes on in subsequent paragraphs to discuss each of the items listed (one per paragraph).

A simple method of checking whether the items in a sentence are parallel is to write them out below each other in a list to see how they compare:

Example

Authors of academic papers should avoid

- an informal style;
- unnecessary wordiness;
- writing a poorly organized paper.

By listing, it becomes clear that the third item in this example is not parallel in structure with the first two. There are various ways of correcting this to produce a better flowing sentence:

Authors of academic papers should avoid an informal style, unnecessary wordiness and poor organization. (*Pattern: adjective-noun*)

or

Academic papers should be formal, concise and well organized. (*Pattern: adjective*)

TASK 1

Make the items in a and b, below, grammatically parallel.

Hint: Try listing the items in order first to identify any differences between them:

---

a. *Modern ports require space for the storage of bulk cargoes, basins large enough to take the ships or terminal jetties at which they can tie up, and an industrial area in which industry can expand.*

b. *Being a student requires motivation; you have to be able to concentrate; you must enjoy hard work.*

TASK 2

Write a parallel sentence for each of the following:

---

a. The lecture was both _____ and _____ .
b. My adviser was not only _____ but also _____ .
c. _____ is more effective than _____ .
d. The research project was _____ conceived, _____ implemented and _____ written up.
e. I was told not only what she said but also _____ .

TASK 3

Write one complete sentence for each of the following using *both . . . and* (or, where possible, *not only . . . but also*) to create a parallel structure:

---

a. experiment
    dangerous
    unreliable

b. Marcel
    student
    time well
    advice

c. a monolingual group
    a bilingual group
    in the study

3.1.2 Sentence combining

Another way of writing clearly and concisely and creating smooth-flowing text is by carefully combining sentences. This can help you to avoid writing short, choppy sentences as well as overly long, unwieldy ones. A series of short, abrupt sentences can indicate an immature writing style, while long, unwieldy sentences often result in poor and/or overly complex sentence structure, making it difficult to read and understand what is written.

There are a number of ways in which sentences can be combined. Used well these can introduce variety into your writing:

- **Coordination** (*and, or, but, yet, so, for*)
  One error many students make when writing academic English is to begin sentences with coordinating conjunctions (*and, or, but, yet, so, for*). As their name suggests, the job of coordinating conjunctions is to join (coordinate) clauses or sentences and as such they can be considered the most basic method of sentence combining. More sophisticated writers will sometimes use 'And' or 'But' (and occasionally 'Yet') to begin the occasional sentence – but you are advised not to do this until you are very confident about your writing style.

Examples

- *Parents are far more lenient with their children nowadays than in the past, so it is not surprising that some children lack discipline and resent authority.*
- *Young people are often influenced by peer pressure, but this, in itself, is not sufficient to explain why some youngsters commit extremely violent crimes.*

- **Conjunctive adverbs** (*moreover, however, therefore, etc.*)
  A more sophisticated way of joining two sentences – one often used in more formal writing – is to form a compound sentence by placing a conjunctive adverb at the beginning or near the beginning of the second sentence. A semi-colon is placed before the conjunction when there is a close relationship between the two sentences (see 'Punctuation Basics' in Part 3, Toolkit); otherwise, a full stop is used (particularly if the sentences are long ones) and the conjunctive adverb begins a new sentence.

Examples

- The environment is now high on the Government's agenda; therefore, plans for wind farms are likely to be received sympathetically.
- Zoos today are facing a number of problems. They are often criticised for keeping wild animals away from their natural habitats and in restrictive enclosures where visitors can gawp at them. Furthermore, many are facing financial difficulties as they receive fewer visitors and face increasing costs. However, the educational value of zoos and their work in protecting species in danger of extinction is often overlooked, particularly by their fiercest critics.

- *Subordinate conjunctions* (*although, because, if, unless, when, whereas*, etc.)
  Complex sentences are formed by using at least one dependent (subordinate) clause, which is introduced by a subordinate conjunction. This subordinate clause either precedes or follows an independent (main) clause.

What is an independent clause? An *independent clause* expresses a complete idea and contains a subject and a verb. Grammatically, it is a complete sentence which can stand alone, hence the term 'independent' clause. Independent clauses can be used as main clauses in longer sentences containing one or more subordinate clauses.

What is a subordinate clause? A *subordinate clause* is introduced by a subordinating word or phrase, such as a subordinating conjunction (*although, despite the fact that* etc.). It does not express a complete idea, so, unlike an independent clause, it cannot stand alone but must always be used with a main clause if it is to express a complete idea, hence the term 'dependent' clause.

When a subordinate clause *begins* a sentence, it is separated by a comma; when it *follows* the main clause, a comma is unnecessary.

Examples

- Whereas a few animal rights' protestors use violence to further their aims, others employ peaceful means in their fight against the cruel treatment and abuse of animals.
- While it will probably never be possible to ban the use of cars in all built-up areas, the provision of a subsidised public transport system with relatively cheap fares will go a long way to reducing congestion and pollution in these areas.

- *Compound-complex sentences*
  These are formed by joining one of (at least) two independent clauses with a dependent clause. A semi-colon is used to separate the complex sentence (see above) from the compound sentence(s) that follow.

Example

- Because the buses were very crowded, we decided to walk (complex sentence); in spite of this, we arrived early (*compound sentence 1*) and had time for a drink before the performance (*compound sentence 2*).
- Although keeping animals in zoos may be the only way to protect endangered species, it is not necessary to keep other exotic wild animals

in captivity (*complex sentence*); therefore, I am of the view that zoos should limit themselves to breeding programmes involving animals who might otherwise face extinction (*compound sentence 1*) <u>and</u> that by doing so they can attract funds from various sources (*compound sentence 2*).

- The majority of respondents to the survey gave traffic congestion as the major reason for their wishing to move away from the area while others gave conflict with neighbours and poor schools as their primary motive.

 Remember that trying to be economical in your writing by combining your sentences, where possible, often will improve your writing style because it forces you to use more sophisticated structures.

TASK 4

Rewrite the following sentences as a paragraph using the above sentence combining techniques to join sentences where appropriate.

1. The Johnson brothers formed a partnership in 1885.
2. Their operations began in New Jersey in the USA the following year.
3. They had 14 employees.
4. They made surgical dressings.
5. In 1887 the company was incorporated.
6. It was called Johnson & Johnson.
7. Sir Joseph Lister was an eminent British surgeon.
8. He had identified airborne germs as a source of infection during operations.
9. Many people were contemptuous of Lister's work.
10. Robert Wood Johnson heard him speak.
11. He decided to create a sterile, wrapped and sealed surgical dressing.
12. The first products were improved medicinal plasters.
13. They contained medical compounds mixed in an adhesive.
14. These were replaced by a soft, absorbent cotton and gauze dressing.
15. This dressing could be mass-produced and shipped in large quantities to hospitals, physicians and chemists.
16. In 1920 another of Johnson & Johnson's famous products was discovered by accident.
17. This was the Band-Aid adhesive bandage.
18. A cotton mill employee was upset.
19. His name was Earle E. Dickson.

20. His young wife kept cutting herself.
21. She did this working in the kitchen.
22. Earle made a ready-to-use bandage.
23. His wife could apply it herself.
24. Today Johnson & Johnson manufacture a wide range of products.
25. These products are designed to meet the needs of healthcare professionals worldwide.
26. The company now employs at least 83,000 people in 52 countries.

(Adapted from Baren 1992)

 TASK KEY

TASK 1 (Possible answers)

a. Modern ports require <u>space to store</u> bulk cargoes, large <u>basins to allow</u> ships to dock or <u>to accommodate</u> terminal jetties for ships to tie up, and an industrial <u>area to allow</u> for the expansion of industry (*nouns followed by infinitives*: note how the same infinitive pattern follows 'or').

b. Being a student requires <u>motivation</u>, <u>concentration</u> and hard <u>work</u>.

TASK 2 (Possible answers)

a. The lecture was both informative and <u>stimulating</u>.
b. My adviser was not only helpful but also understanding.
c. <u>Increasing</u> interest rates is more effective than <u>keeping</u> wage rates down.
d. I was told not only <u>what you said</u> but also <u>what you implied</u>.

TASK 3 (Possible answers)

a. The experiment is both dangerous and unreliable.
   or
   The experiment is not only dangerous but also unreliable.
b. Marcel is a student who both manages his time well and listens to/acts on advice.
   or
   Marcel is a student who not only manages his time well, but also listens to/ acts on advice.
c. Both a monolingual (group) and a bilingual group were compared in the study.
   (*Not only . . . but also* is inappropriate here because it lays too strong an emphasis on the second item when both items are of equal value).

TASK 4   (Possible answer)

The Johnson Brothers formed a partnership in 1885 and operations began in New Jersey in the USA the following year with 14 employees, who made surgical dressings. In 1887, the company, called Johnson & Johnson, was incorporated. Sir Joseph Lister, an eminent British surgeon, had identified airborne germs as a source of infection during operations. While many people were contemptuous of Lister's work, Robert Wood Johnson, who had heard him speak, decided to create a sterile, wrapped and sealed surgical dressing. The first products, which were improved medicinal plasters, contained medical compounds mixed in an adhesive. These were later replaced by a soft, absorbent cotton and gauze dressing that could be mass-produced and shipped in large quantities to hospitals, physicians and chemists. In 1920, another of Johnson & Johnson's famous products, the Band-Aid adhesive bandage, was discovered by accident. A cotton mill employee, Earle E. Dickson, was upset because his young wife kept cutting herself while working in the kitchen. Earle therefore decided to make a ready-to-use bandage that his wife could apply herself. Today Johnson & Johnson manufacture a wide range of products that are designed to meet the needs of healthcare professionals worldwide. The company now employs at least 83,000 people in 52 countries.

3.2 Level of formality (register)

One thing that distinguishes academic writing from other types of writing is its level of formality, sometimes called 'register'. Academic writing requires a more formal style that can be seen in:

a. *the type of vocabulary used*: although, as we have seen, it is important not to make your writing unnecessarily complex, nevertheless in academic writing there are certain words that may often be preferable to their more casual counterparts. Here are just a few commonly used examples:

saw/noticed → observed
shows   → illustrates, indicates
so   → therefore, consequently
but   → however, nevertheless, although
people   → subjects
big   → large, considerable, substantial
long   → extensive, extended
seems   → appears
important   → significant

b. *the avoidance of first person singular ('I')*: this is another example of how ideas about good style change. Traditionally, it was not acceptable to use 'I' in academic writing; however, this is beginning to change and increasingly the word 'I' is appearing in course assignments and research reports. This is true of some disciplines more than others and we would therefore advise you to check with your department, tutor or supervisor what the appropriate practice is in your own field. Nevertheless, it remains true that in general it is preferable to avoid using 'I'. When in doubt, play safe and do what tradition dictates.

This raises the question of which alternative forms you can use instead of 'I'. In other words, how can you de-personalise your language? Figure 3.1 shows some examples of ways writers typically depersonalize their writing.

PERSONAL	IMPERSONAL
I	*The author/This writer*
I found that ...	*It was found that ...*
I was surprised to observe that ...	*The observation that ... was surprising.*
I found the results interesting because ...	*The results were interesting in that ...*
I decided to use ...	*The decision was made to use ...*
I think/believe that ...	*It might be argued that ...*
	It would seem reasonable to argue that ...
I take this to mean	*This suggests/indicates that ...*
	This can be taken to mean that ...

FIGURE 3.1 How writers depersonalize their writing

You will notice from the examples given in the figure that a common strategy for depersonalizing language is to change the active voice (on the left) to the passive voice (on the right).

c. *absence of slang and other more casual forms*: slang is normally not used in academic writing, unless of course the language itself is the focus of attention, as it might be in the case of a study on literature or linguistics, for example. It is not always easy for students, particularly non-native speakers of English, to know what is and is not slang, particularly as slang is becoming increasingly pervasive in most written and spoken genres. It is therefore a good idea to check any language you are uncertain about. And, again, you should ensure that your finished thesis is checked for inappropriate language by a native speaker.

d. *absence of contracted forms*: contracted forms are usually associated with an informal writing style. It is best to avoid using contracted forms in academic writing; instead use complete forms (e.g. "it is" *not* "it's"; "that is" *not* "that's"; "they are" *not* "they're"; "result is" not "result's"). An exception to this rule concerns the quoting of subjects. For example, if subjects used in your study have provided written data, then you should record it exactly as it was given to you, contractions and all. Similarly, when transcribing (recording in writing) spoken data such as interviews, you have a duty to do this as accurately as possible and you may therefore need to use contracted forms.

3.3 Using Gender-neutral language

Increasingly, students are required to use gender-neutral language in their written work, whether it is a research report or coursework. It is best, therefore, to avoid the use of *he* and *she* wherever possible, unless of course it refers to specific individuals cited in your thesis/dissertation.

Examples

Instead of *Before a researcher embarks on fieldwork, he needs to ensure that he has adequate funding.*

write: *Before a researcher embarks on fieldwork, they need to ensure that they have adequate funding.*

or

Before researchers embark on fieldwork, they need to ensure that they have adequate funding.

Instead of *If a sociologist is to make generalizations, she needs to do so responsibly.*

write: *If sociologists are to make generalizations, they need to do so responsibly.*

or *If a sociologist is to make generalizations, he or she needs to do so responsibly.*
(**Note:** '*he*' or '*she*' is sometimes written as '*he/she*' or '*s/he*'; however, we would caution against overuse of this convention.)
or *Sociologists who make generalizations need to do so responsibly.*

3.4 Reading other research projects

Finally, try to look at dissertations and theses that have been written by other people. This will help you develop a sense of what is and is not good style, and of what is and is not appropriate and acceptable. Remember, much of what we learn about good style we learn from reading. The principles explained in this book will help you develop good style, in part by enabling you to recognize it when you see it applied in the course of your reading. This process will sensitize you to the requirements of academic writing in general and research-report writing in particular, and ultimately empower you to improve your own writing.

4

Approaching your writing project: tips and strategies

4.1 Planning carefully • 4.2 Deciding on your writing approach • 4.3 Sourcing and selecting information • 4.4 Recording information/ making notes • 4.5 Drafting • 4.6 Defining terms • 4.7 Supporting your claims • 4.8 Acknowledging alternative perspectives and counter-arguments

As with any major project, if you are to complete your assignment or research report successfully and efficiently you need to be highly disciplined, organized and methodical. All too often, failure to complete a written academic project – and a research project in particular – is the result of a lack of discipline which leads to it dragging on, the student losing interest and a sense of continuity, and the project losing its freshness and becoming outdated and irrelevant as developments in the field overtake it.

The following strategies will help you achieve discipline during the planning and writing up of your work and thus increase greatly your chances of successfully completing your course and/or degree. Some of the strategies apply more particularly to the writing up of research projects, but most apply to all academic writing.

4.1 Planning carefully

This involves organizing your time carefully and setting yourself milestones by which you attempt to achieve certain goals. In other words, set yourself deadlines for completing particular sections of your assignment or research report. These goals could, for example, be finishing your literature review or introduction, finishing a particular section or chapter, concluding your data collection, completing your analysis, completing a first draft of your assignment, dissertation or thesis, or even overcoming a particular problem you have come up against. You will, of course, fail at times to achieve your goals, but that does not really matter; what matters is that by creating milestones and setting goals you place demands on yourself and in doing so help ensure that your assignment or report progresses. Setting milestones is a good way of keeping up momentum and preventing your project from getting 'bogged down'. Most importantly, perhaps, if your project has momentum you will feel motivated!

 By being organized in this way you also make it easier for your tutor or supervisor to monitor your progress, and therefore to be of greater assistance to you.

4.2 Deciding on your writing approach

How you approach the writing of your assignment or research report will depend partly on your personality and style of working, and partly on the nature of the project itself. Some people prefer to begin writing almost immediately, continually adjusting and refining their work as they go along, until they eventually produce a final, acceptable draft. Others prefer to leave the writing-up until the final phase, by which time they will likely have copious notes and a very clear idea of what the final product will look like. Both approaches have advantages and disadvantages.

4.2.1 Writing from the start

This approach has the following advantages and disadvantages.

Advantages

- The very process of writing can help to generate ideas and clarify your thinking.
- It can be motivating as it gives you a real sense of progress.
- Each piece of writing that you do can be used to generate and guide discussion during meetings with your tutor or supervisor.

Disadvantages

- This approach lends itself less to empirically based research than to purely theoretical research. In the case of empirically based research, what you can write of the thesis will be more subject to constraints imposed by the processes of data collection and analysis. This will often mean a delay in the writing of significant parts of the thesis.
- You will often discard (sometimes large) sections of your writing as your ideas develop and change.
- Because research work in particular often evolves significantly over time, you are unlikely to have a definite idea of the structure of your report until fairly late on. Indeed, it is not uncommon to end up with a structure that is quite different from what you anticipated when you first embarked on your research.

4.2.2 Writing as the final phase

This approach has the following advantages and disadvantages.

Advantages

- When you begin writing you have a very clear idea about the precise structure of your assignment/research report.
- Your thinking will have been clarified and most conceptual difficulties will have been resolved with the result that you are likely to spend less time on 'wasted' writing.
- You will be able to focus almost entirely on the process of writing rather than on the clarification and analysis of ideas and data.

Disadvantages

- If you face problems with the collection and/or analysis of data, you may feel as though you are making little or no progress. This can weaken motivation and lead to your project getting bogged down and losing the momentum necessary to bring it to a successful conclusion.
- Sometimes problems associated with research only come to light during the writing process, when you are focusing more intently on what you are

saying and how you can best express it. Those problems *may* have major implications for the whole project, especially if they suggest the methodology used is flawed. If you leave your writing up to the final stage of the project, it may be very difficult to make major revisions so late in the day in order to rectify such problems.

Whichever approach you adopt, it is important that you make your decision early on according to the nature of your particular assignment or research project and your working style.

4.3 Sourcing and selecting information

The information you include in your work may come from a variety of different sources. Some of these will be oral, and some written.

4.3.1 Oral sources of information

- Lectures;
- seminars/research seminars;
- conference presentations;
- professional organizations and Special Interest Groups (SIGs).

Oral sources of information have limited credibility as they are frequently undocumented; consequently, they should be used sparingly and their limited value as oral sources acknowledged. If, however, ideas expressed at a conference presentation, for example, appear subsequently in a publication of the 'conference proceedings', these can be cited more confidently as they are documented and therefore constitute a more legitimate and credible source.

4.3.2 Written sources of information

- Journals;
- books;
- references found in books and journal articles, either in the main text, bibliography or 'recommended readings' sections;
- conference proceedings.

4.3.3 Electronic sources of information

- The internet;
- on-line services.

The quantity, quality and accessibility of on-line services is constantly improving, and your university's Information Services and Systems (or its equivalent) will be able to give you detailed advice on the services available to you and how to use and get the most out of them. Here, we will give you a brief indication of the kinds of electronic resources available to you, but suggest that you consult with the relevant department at your university in order to obtain more detailed information.

British Humanities Index (BHInet): as its name suggests, this database focuses on research in the humanities and as such covers subjects such as the arts, literature, cinema, economics, history, current affairs, popular science, religion, music, and architecture. It indexes over 300 internationally respected journals and weekly magazines published in the UK from 1962 to the present, and is updated monthly.

Web of Knowledge: this is a citation and journal database which gives access to the following resources:

- *Web of Science* comprising 3 databases: Arts and Humanities Citation Index, Science Citation Index, and Social Sciences Citation Index. It provides over 30 million references to research from over 9000 journals.
- *Arts and Humanities Citation Index* which indexes articles in the arts and humanities from over 1400 journals from 1975 to the present. Subject areas include philosophy, history, language, linguistics, music, literature, religion, theatre, and the visual arts.
- *Social Sciences Citation Index* covering nearly 1800 journals across disciplines from 1956 onwards. Subject areas include political science, women's studies, European studies, history, philosophy of science, anthropology, ethics, and applied linguistics.
- *ISI Proceedings – Social Sciences and Humanities* which indexes the published literature of the most significant conferences, symposia and seminars from 1990 to date. Subject areas covered include art, history, literature and philosophy.
- *Journal Citation Reports* providing citation data showing high impact and frequency of use from 1997 onwards in subjects such as political science, women's studies, European studies, history, philosophy of science, anthropology, ethics, and applied linguistics.

OCLC FirstSearch: this is a gateway to databases, eJournals, eBooks, and archived content. Databases include ATLA Religion (with references to journal articles, book reviews, and collections of essays in all scholarly fields of religion since 1949, featuring articles written in 36 languages), ClasePeriodica (with citations from Latin American journals in the sciences, social sciences and humanities from 1975), Modern Languages Association (MLA) Bibliography (with references to journal articles on literature, modern languages and linguistics from 1926), and RILM Music Abstracts (with a bibliography of scholarship on music and related disciplines from 1967).

Access to database resources such as the British Humanities Index, Web of Knowledge and OCLC FirstSearch is normally made through your academic institution's Library and Learning Services website. Most universities will have a licence to use these databases which in turn will allow its staff and students free access to them. In the case of the BHI, for instance, this should be listed as a database on your university's LLS website. Selecting it will take you to the 'CSA Illumina' page which contains a complete list of databases held by CSA. From that list you can select those you are interested in, including the BHI. For further information, we suggest that you contact your university library in the first instance. They should be able to give you further, more detailed guidance on which resources are available to you and how you can access them.

Other Databases: what follows is a list of some other widely used databases. The British Library provides a useful, more comprehensive list which can be found at the following address: http://www.bl.uk/collections/wider/elecsubaz5.html#letterr:

- Anthropology Plus;
- Applied Social Sciences Index and Abstracts (ASSIA);
- Archive of Americana;
- Bibliografia de la Literatura Española;
- Bibliographie de Civilisation Médiévale;
- Bibliography of American Literature;
- Bibliography of the History of Art;
- British Newspaper Index;
- Central and Eastern European Online Library;
- Dictionary of Old English Corpus;
- Early English Books Online (EEBO);
- Eighteenth Century Collections Online (ECCO, multidisciplinary);
- French Bibliography 15th Century;
- Grove Art Online;
- Grove Music Online;
- Handbook of Latin American Studies Online;
- Hispanic American Periodicals Index (HAPI);
- Index to Theses (covering theses accepted in Great Britain and Northern Ireland since 1716);
- International Bibliography of the Social Sciences;
- International Medieval Bibliography;
- International Philosophical Bibliography;
- Library of Latin Texts (CLCLT);
- Linguistics and Language Behavior Abstracts (LLBA);

- Literature Resource Center;
- Middle English Compendium;
- Oxford English Dictionary;
- Oxford Reference Online;
- Oxford Scholarship Online;
- Philosopher's Index;
- Russian National Bibliography;
- Russian/NIS Universal Databases;
- Social Policy and Practice;
- Sociological Abstracts;
- Times Digital Archive;
- Victorian Database Online;
- ZETOC (British Library Electronic Table of Contents).

(See also Sections 2.3 and 6.12 for specific tips on using electronic sources.)

4.3.4 Keeping up to date

If your work is to be current and relevant it is important that you keep up to date with the latest information. While this can be a difficult task, there are now electronically based 'current awareness services' that are designed to help make it easier. Active current awareness services use email to alert you to new print or electronic resources as they are published. Passive services can be consulted periodically by visiting a web page for the latest information. Services include:

- discussion lists and newsgroups;
- funding alerts;
- journal alerting;
- monitoring web-page changes (particularly important for referencing);
- new publications;
- news of forthcoming conferences;
- news services with email alerting.

4.4 Recording information/making notes

As you read your sources, you will need to identify, highlight and record relevant information. There are a variety of note-taking techniques that can help you do this efficiently.

4.4.1 Identifying relevant information

Although there will be times when you will need to read complete texts, there will be many other times when you will be reading an article, book and so on simply to find out whether it contains particular information. This is called *scanning*. The following strategies can help you in this task:

- Look for key words associated with the ideas or information you are seeking.
- Look for the names of scholars/writers associated with the ideas or information you are seeking.
- Look for the titles of books, articles and so on associated with the ideas or information you are seeking.
- Read abstracts of articles. These will give you a *synopsis* (summary) of the content of the article. In the case of a website search, the results will often include a brief description or introduction to, or sample sentences from the website.
- Read the information found in the prefaces and on the back covers of books.
- Look through tables of contents.
- Look through indexes.

4.4.2 Indicating relevant information

- Underlining or marking relevant information in the margin.
- Photocopying or scanning, and then highlighting the relevant information.
- In the case of information sourced from a website, you can either (a) copy the relevant information into a word document, or (b) copy the complete web page and later indicate the relevant passages by highlighting, bolding, underlining or italicising them, or by changing the colour of the relevant text.

4.4.3 Recording relevant information

There are many different ways of ordering the information you gather, and every individual has their own personal and sometimes unique way of doing this; there are, however, a few general techniques that can improve your speed and efficiency.

4.4.3.1 Distinguishing main and supporting ideas

One good way of doing this is to organize information on the page in the way suggested in 'Main and Supporting Ideas' (Section 2.2): write main ideas on the left of your notepaper, and then offset supporting ideas to the right. Another method is to use spidergrams such as the example featured in Figure 4.1. In this case, the title of the chapter, book or article, along with its author

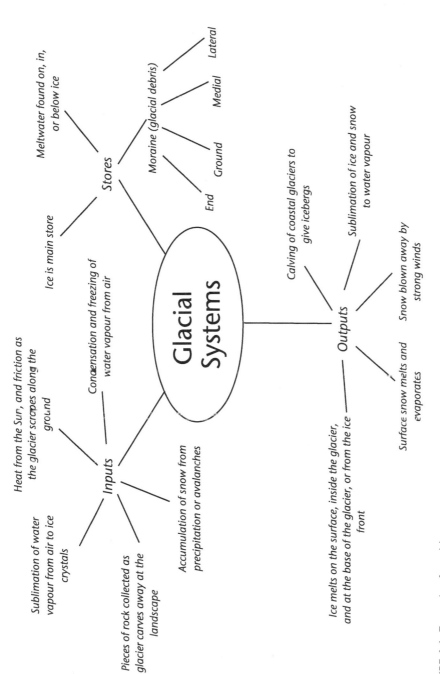

FIGURE 4.1 Example of a spidergram.

and date, is written in the centre of the spidergram. The first 'layer' of lines emanating out from the centre contains the main ideas, and lines emanating out from those first lines to form a second 'layer' are the supporting ideas. In other words, the lines furthest from the centre of the diagram contain more focused and detailed information. You therefore create a visual map of the material you are reading, a graphic representation of the hierarchy of ideas it contains. By drawing lines between different branches of the diagram you can signal connections between ideas, some of which may occur to you as you are reading or when you have finished note-taking and are considering the content of your notes.

Hierarchies of ideas or argument structures can also be indicated using numbering and/or lettering systems. Look at the following example:

```
I   i    a b c
    ii   a b
II  i    a b c d
III i    a b
    ii   a b c
    iii  a b c
```

Here there are three main ideas (I–III), each of which has a number of supporting ideas (i, ii or iii), and further supporting details or perhaps less important information (a, b, c and d). In other words, numbering and lettering systems can, like the layout of information and spidergrams, indicate the status of information, from core to more peripheral and general to more specific.

 These kinds of organizational maps are also a useful way of planning your own writing.

TASK 1

Using a journal article, a chapter from a book, or a piece of your own writing, identify and record the main and supporting ideas with the help of one of the above hierarchies.

4.4.3.2 Arranging notes to reflect the layout of an article or book

This can be done using chapter numbers, titles, headings and sub-headings.

4.4.3.3 Using a working outline or skeleton of your project

When you find information relevant to a particular section of your assignment or research report, write it into the outline in note form. As you read further material, you can add additional information to the outline or use a fresh outline for each book, chapter, article and so on that you read.

4.4.3.4 Detailing your sources clearly

As you note down information, remember to include its source and the page number(s) where it appeared.

 Try to be very methodical in recording your sources. Trying to remember and locate your sources later on can be very difficult, time consuming and frustrating. As many students have found to their cost, it is far better to spend time noting down sources when you first locate them than to waste three times as much time hunting them down later!

4.4.3.5 Using abbreviations

Where possible use abbreviations such as the following:

e.g.	for example	i.e.	that is; in other words
etc.	et cetera; and so on	vs.	versus; in contrast to

You can also abbreviate long words and names by using the first syllable or initials:

temp = temperature	H.C. = Hamish Chandler
ptt = plate tectonics	g-therm = geothermal
fb = feedback	cont drift = continental drift

4.4.3.6 Using symbols

Where possible, use symbols as substitutes for complete words or phrases. The following symbols are commonly used by students:

=	equals; is the same as	≠	does not equal/is not the same as
>	is more than/larger than	<	is less than/smaller than
∴	therefore; as a result	∵	*or* cos because
↑	to increase	↓	to decrease
→	leads to; causes	←	is caused by; depends on

[includes	] excludes
+ *or* & and	. . . continues; etc.
£/$ pounds/dollars	% percent

4.4.3.7 Using simple sketches or diagrams

A picture really can be worth a thousand words! Look at the following example:

World recession and low interest rates encourage LEDCs to borrow heavily from the World Bank and other sources to finance their industrial development. However, as interest rates increase, LEDCs find themselves in more debt as they are not able to pay the interest. Rising debts mean many LEDCs have no money to invest in agriculture and industry, so development slows down. Therefore, further loans are required, meaning that the only way out of the cycle is for lenders to cancel debts.

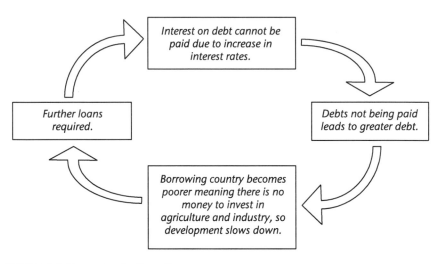

FIGURE 4.2 Example of a flow diagram.

(Adapted from Coordination Group Publications Ltd., 2003)

 Be sure to number your sketches and diagrams for easy reference; 'Figure 1', 'Figure 2' and so on are normally used.

4.5 Drafting

Once you have finished selecting and recording information, and you have your own thoughts clarified, you will probably want to begin drafting. Drafting means writing a rough first copy of your assignment or research report (or a part of it), which you will edit and refine later. You may end up writing two or even three drafts before you feel the report is polished enough for submission to your tutors or examiners.

Drafting is a crucial part of the writing process for the following reasons:

- It is very rare for writers to produce their best work at the first attempt.
- Your ideas may change or develop during or after the writing of your first draft. You may, for example, have come across a recently published book containing new and important information that is relevant to your project.
- You may notice errors in your thinking. There may, for example, be inconsistencies or logical errors that only become evident as you write, or when you read through the complete text.
- You may think of ways to improve the organization of the text to make it more coherent, fluent and easier to read. This could include altering the way you have sectioned the assignment/report, modifying the title and/or section headings and so on.
- There may be grammatical errors that need correcting or stylistic weaknesses that require adjustments to phrasing, vocabulary and so on
- You may decide to improve the visual presentation of your work by making changes to the format of the text. For example, you may wish to alter the system you have used to number the various sections, or to adjust your use of bold and italic typefaces, colour, graphics and so on.
- You may simply have forgotten to include information – points of analysis, quotations, graphics, data and so on.
- Drafting helps you become more familiar with your work and with its strengths and weaknesses. Particularly if you are pursuing a PhD degree, this can be very useful preparation for the oral defence of your thesis (the 'viva').

 The above points can be used as a checklist when reading your draft(s).

How and when you draft and rewrite will of course depend to some extent on the approach you take to writing up your work (see strategy 2 above). If you leave your writing up to the final phase, then the drafting-rewriting process will very likely be different to that of the person who begins writing early on and constantly engages in the process of drafting and rewriting as he or she works on each section of their assignment/research report. If you begin writing from early on, your ideas are still developing and are therefore not fully formed; consequently, you will end up doing a good deal of drafting and rewriting 'as you go along' and as your thinking changes and develops. However, whichever approach you choose to take, you will always need eventually to read your work in full and to rewrite parts of it. Only when you view it in its entirety will you get a real sense of how well it reads and how coherent it is.

4.6 Defining terms

Defining terms means explaining them – in much the same way that a dictionary explains the meaning of a word. In academic writing, however, definitions may well be much longer, more in-depth and more complex than those found in a dictionary because the concepts and ideas they explain will often be more complex and the subject of controversy and speculation.

You must remember to define clearly any terminology you use in your assignment/research report. The following simple rules can help you in deciding what you should regard as 'terminology' and therefore which words, concepts and ideas you should define.

- Define any key terms; in other words, terms that are central to your work, are somewhat specialised, and occur frequently.
- Define any terms that have a particular meaning in your field of study which is different and distinct from any general meaning they may have when used elsewhere.
- Define any specialized language that is unique to your field of study and is not found elsewhere.
- Define any terms whose meanings have become unclear as the result of different writers defining and employing them differently.

Clearly, defining terms is crucial to achieving clarity and avoiding ambiguity. Any potential ambiguity can seriously undermine your work by leaving it vulnerable to (deliberate or accidental) misinterpretation. As with all aspects of your writing, you *must* close off any possible avenues of criticism and produce something which is as 'water-tight' as possible.

One of the golden rules of research report writing is to pre-empt criticism by being highly explicit and openly acknowledging any potential failings or shortcomings in your research, where possible explaining why they could not be overcome in this instance and how they might be overcome in any future studies. Again, anticipation is a key strategy in helping neutralise criticism, and it includes being rigorous in your definition of terms.

4.7 Supporting your claims

In our discussion of argument in writing and paragraph structure (Sections 1.7 and 2.2), the importance of supporting ideas in academic writing was considered briefly. When writing up your work you need to be especially aware of the need to support *any* claims you make with adequate evidence. Unless it is self-evident or common knowledge, you cannot simply make a bold statement and expect your readers to accept it in the absence of good evidence. Remember: unsupported statements are another invitation for criticism, for they undermine the rigour and value of your argument, and they suggest a writer who is naïve and/or undisciplined in the conventions and requirements of good scholarship.

Evidence can come in one or more different forms, including the following:

- Quotations from or paraphrase of the work of respected scholars. Less well known scholars *may* suffice but you will need to be discriminating; the more crucial or fundamental your argument, and the stronger the claims you are making, the more respected the scholar(s) you are quoting will need to be.
- Rational exposition/argument showing the validity of any claims you make. As we have seen, well-structured, logical argument is a powerful weapon when handled with skill and care.
- Empirical data that have been documented or which have emerged from your own research.

Avoid using anecdotal evidence or hearsay to support your arguments. It is unscientific and so of little value unless there is documentary evidence you can draw on to back it up.

Equally, try to avoid generalizations. Many generalizations are suspect, and even those that are not tend to be of little value. Any generalizations you chose to make or cite in your writing need to be widely recognized as reasonably sound or 'valid' and preferably well documented in scholarly or quasi-scholarly literature. While generalizations should be treated with caution by all those engaged in academic discourse, it is especially true of researchers, who need and are expected to be demonstrably 'scientific' and precise in their approach.

4.7.1 Using tentative language to show reservation or uncertainty

If you are uncertain of any claims you make, it is important that this uncertainty is reflected in your language, which needs to be more tentative in order to indicate the 'insecure' status of what you are saying. The following expressions can help you achieve this:

There is evidence to suggest that . . .
There is some evidence that . . .
On this basis, it could be argued that . . .
This offers limited support for the view that . . .

One might tentatively conclude that . . .
There are indications that . . .
This might be taken as indicating at least that . . .
This might be seen as supporting the notion that . . .

4.8 Acknowledging alternative perspectives and counter-arguments

Any good academic needs to have integrity and to be as objective about their work as possible, whether they are producing a course assignment, a PhD thesis or a journal article. This means acknowledging and respecting the views, approaches, perspectives, and findings of other scholars, even when these conflict with their own. In the case of a research report, acknowledging the views of others shows that you are familiar with the literature relevant to your own study and provides your own research with greater credibility by contextualizing it more fully and showing that you have taken into account all possible views when designing, carrying out and analysing your research. In other words, you are providing as balanced and complete a picture as possible and thereby also allowing your readers to make more informed judgements about your own research and the spirit in which you have conducted it. If you do mention other views, approaches and findings that conflict with your own, you will need to provide a clear rationale explaining either why the differences are unimportant or perhaps irrelevant, or why they are less suitable or credible than those you have chosen to adopt.

Finally, by acknowledging the views of other scholars you are again protecting yourself from the possible criticism that you are giving a one-sided picture and ignoring views or data that do not suit your purposes. Regardless of whether you are completing an essay or a PhD thesis, it is better to get things out into the open and to address them directly, while they are under your control, than risk the reproaches of your lecturer or the examiner.

Part 2

PUTTING TOGETHER YOUR RESEARCH PROJECT

5

Understanding the research and writing process

5.1 What is a research project? • 5.2 What's the difference between a dissertation and a thesis? • 5.3 The basic requirements of a research degree • 5.4 Deciding on a research topic • 5.5 Choosing and using your Supervisor: what exactly is their role? • 5.6 Writing a proposal • 5.7 Adopting the correct mindset • 5.8 Studying independently • 5.9 Attending research seminars, conferences etc. • 5.10 Understanding disciplinary differences • 5.11 The upgrading process (PhDs only) • 5.12 Familiarity with 'Codes of Practice'/Rules and Regulations • 5.13 Ethical considerations • 5.14 The Importance of finding your own 'voice' . . . and why it can be challenging • 5.15 Getting down to writing

5.1 What is a research project?

In this guide, we have used the term 'research project' to refer to that component of a degree programme which requires you, the student, to successfully design, conduct and write up a piece of research as a condition of being awarded the degree. In the vast majority of cases that research will form either a dissertation or a thesis.

5.2 What is the difference between a dissertation and a thesis?

Students are often unclear about the difference between a dissertation and a thesis. For the purpose of this writing guide, there are no significant differences between the two in as much as both apply the same general principles of academic writing style and share similar principles of structure, organization and formatting. Where they differ is in their respective levels of detail: because a dissertation is normally one of a number of written requirements of a Bachelors or Masters degree (BA, BSc, MA, MSc. MEd. or MPhil) it will typically be shorter in length and less detailed and far-reaching. In contrast, a thesis is the sole written requirement for the PhD degree and constitutes the final product of a lengthy period of research (normally 3 years or more); as such, it is expected to be considerably longer, more detailed, and more far-reaching than a dissertation. Furthermore, a defining characteristic of a thesis is its originality and the fact that it adds significantly to the existing body of knowledge in the field with which it is concerned. While a dissertation will also involve original work, there is less emphasis on this aspect, and research that replicates a previous study, for example – perhaps in a slightly different context or by employing a slightly different methodology – may well be acceptable.

Finally, a word about the MPhil degree: the Master of Philosophy degree can be a taught degree or a research-based degree. If it is a taught degree, the research project will form one of a number of written assignments that will need to be submitted and assessed before the degree is awarded. As such it will constitute a dissertation. In the case of a research-based MPhil degree, there will be little or no coursework and the research project will become the main focus of your attention and the main subject of assessment. In this case, it will constitute a thesis, reflecting as it does a PhD, if in a more truncated form.

Before looking in detail at the process of actually writing a research report, let's look briefly at a number of general principles and procedures that can help you understand better the whole research process and orientate you to the task ahead. An understanding of these will help smooth your journey over the coming months by increasing your overall awareness as well as the effectiveness and efficiency with which you work. Unfortunately, all too often students learn these principles and procedures the hard way, through experience, and as a result the process of conducting research and producing a dissertation or thesis becomes far more taxing and fraught with difficulties than it needs to be. Many of the following suggestions have to do with thinking ahead, working systematically, and using all the resources at your disposal.

5.3 The basic requirements of a research degree

5.3.1 What is originality?

As we have seen, one of the defining characteristics of a thesis – and to a lesser extent a dissertation – is its originality. In both cases it is a requirement that the research you report on is original. But what does this mean? Simply, that your research must add something new to the body of knowledge that already exists in the field of study in which you are working. It must shed fresh light on that field in a way that no one else has done and in so doing push the barriers of our understanding of it. However, in the case of a dissertation, that contribution to knowledge will, in all probability, be less substantial than that of a thesis; nevertheless, both should seek to offer something new and original.

Here's how one university *Handbook of Academic Regulations for Research Degrees* puts it, 'The thesis shall form a distinct contribution to the knowledge of the subject and afford evidence of originality by the discovery of new facts and/or by the exercise of independent critical power'.

Students often ask the question, 'Just *how* original does the research need to be?' Unfortunately, this is a bit like asking how long a piece of string is. There have undoubtedly been cases where research students have produced work that has completely upended their field and changed the way people think about it. Such change will often be the result of a broad and quite fundamental reassessment of the state of their discipline or key aspects of it, and it may well result ultimately in a complete paradigm shift. However, these cases are few and far between and it is far more common for research students to focus on one (often quite narrow) aspect of their field – we've all heard of the doctoral student who spent 15 years of their life studying the mating habits of an organism barely visible to the human eye! Of course, small doesn't necessarily mean insignificant, and perhaps this realization is key to answering this question: 'Original' means original, regardless of the *reach* of your research and the potential *scale* of its implications. More important than either reach or scale is significance. The examiners – as well as the wider audience (academic or otherwise) – need to feel that your research is significant or worthwhile in the sense that it 'contributes to the knowledge of the subject'. As the earlier quotation makes clear, this can be either through the discovery of new facts and/or the exercise of independent critical power; and, as we have seen, the contribution may consist of shedding light on one minute aspect of a very large field.

5.3.2 Other requirements

Apart from originality, there are other requirements you will need to meet if you are to bring your research to a successful conclusion. It is important you are aware of these requirements *before* embarking on your project and as such we have listed for you a typical set of such requirements – written in rather formal language!

The thesis shall

- consist of the candidate's own account of his/her investigations, the greater proportion of which shall have been undertaken during the period of registration under supervision for the degree;
- be an integrated whole and present a coherent argument;
- give a critical assessment of the relevant literature, describe the method of research and its findings, include discussion on those findings and indicate in what respects they appear to the candidate to advance the study of the subject; and, in doing so, demonstrate a deep and synoptic understanding of the field of study (the candidate being able to place the thesis in a wider context), objectivity and the capacity for judgement in complex situations and autonomous work in that field;
- be written in English and the literary presentation shall be satisfactory, although the candidate, with the support of the supervisor, may make application for a thesis in the field of modern languages and literatures only to be written in the language of study, to be considered on an exceptional basis by the Research Degrees Board of Examiners with advice sought from the Subject Area Board in the Humanities; in such cases the thesis shall include additionally a submission of between 10,000 and 20,000 words which shall be written in English and shall summarize the main arguments of the thesis;
- not exceed 100,000 words (inclusive of footnotes but exclusive of appendices and bibliography, the word limit not applying to editions of a text or texts);
- include a full bibliography and references;
- demonstrate research skills relevant to the thesis being presented;
- be of a standard to merit publication in whole or in part or in a revised form (for example, as a monograph or as a number of articles in learned journals).

 Although the above guidelines relate specifically to a thesis, they apply equally to a dissertation, with the exception of word length which is substantially less in the case of a dissertation – typically 10,000–20,000 words. The word limits for both theses and dissertations can vary from one institution to another and even between departments of the same institution.

5.4 Deciding on a research topic

Although some students decide to embark on a research project as a result of having come across an issue, problem or phenomenon that they wish to investigate, frequently things happen the other way round: a student has decided they would like to conduct research, but they are undecided on what the focus of that research should be. This can be frustrating, for as they read the literature of their field, attend conferences and talk with friends, colleagues and professors in the hope of homing in on a possible subject, there is often a feeling that time is passing and they will never succeed in identifying a suitable topic. What's more, for overseas students holding visas and already studying in the foreign country and paying high tuition fees, the stakes can be especially high as delays in progressing with their research can be very costly.

Here are a few tips on selecting a research topic:

1. Select something you find interesting. While this may sound obvious, all too often research students choose a topic not because they have a genuine interest in it but because they know it will respond to a vacuum which exists in their field of study, or because, if conducted successfully, it could potentially carry them onto the world academic stage. When choosing the focus of your study, you need to bear in mind that it will become a central part of your life for at least the next few months, and probably three years or more in the case of a PhD thesis. It is therefore important that you feel inspired by it enough to carry you through that period without losing momentum.

2. Unless it is to be your life's work – or a good part of it – try to avoid projects that seem open-ended; instead choose something that will fit into the time-scale you have in mind for your research. It may be, for example, that you have set a time limit based on the stipulations of a scholarship scheme or the desire to apply for a promotion or university job that is conditional upon your having experience of conducting research or holding a research degree. In other words, although some people are driven to undertake lengthy and ambitious research projects by romantic notions of dedicating their life's work to producing (ultimately) something earth-shaking, in the majority of cases there are usually more practical constraints and motivations at work, and these will often require you to think carefully about your project and to consider how do-able it is within a particular time limit. Also, be aware that nowadays universities are increasingly requiring students to complete their research projects within a specified period, partly for the students' own sakes, but also to increase degree completion rates. Needless to say, in the case of dissertations, these projects typically will have to be submitted according to a strict deadline in order to be awarded the Bachelors or Masters degree.

3. Areas of controversy and/or areas where there are various views and approaches that allow for comparison are often fertile territory for research. Good research, while it may not resolve disputes, can nevertheless play an important role in helping clarify issues. A word of caution though: opting to conduct research in a highly controversial area or one which is well off the 'beaten track', while having the potential to make an impact and give you prominence as a researcher, can also prove to be a dead-end in terms of your research career. A research area or topic may be unexplored simply because it is not very significant in the broader scheme of things or because other people are not interested in it!

4. Similarly, a recent breakthrough in a field can frequently generate ideas for further 'spin-off' research projects. Keep up to speed, therefore, with the latest developments in your area of study.

5. Discuss developments in your field and areas of particular interest to you with fellow students, colleagues and lecturers. Sometimes it may also be possible to talk through possibilities with your potential supervisor; if they know you well and recognize your potential, they may even suggest a focus for your research or invite you to investigate a specific research question under their supervision.

6. Finally, try to be alert to potential research leads. Often these will reveal themselves through the media, seminars, workshops, your own reading and personal experience, or at conferences. Most students looking for a research topic become increasingly 'switched on' to possible avenues of investigation in the sense that this quest is at the forefront of their minds; they are sensitive to suggestions of topics and therefore tend to recognize them when they arise. Try to enter that mindset yourself.

5.5 Choosing and using your supervisor: what exactly is their role?

Depending on the type of degree you are working towards, you may need a dedicated supervisor; this is especially true of postgraduate degrees, and in particular the MPhil and PhD. In the case of undergraduate and Masters' dissertations, you may well be assigned a tutor or supervisor according to your research topic or tutor group, and consequently may not be in a position to choose your research tutor/supervisor. Indeed, this is sometimes even true in the case of research projects for more advanced degrees. Assuming, however, that you are in a position to choose your supervisor, selecting the right person can make or break your research project, so it is important that you get it right. There are a number of questions you will want to ask yourself the answers to which will influence your decision. These include:

- *Do they have the necessary expertise in the area that will be the focus of my research?*
Although it is not necessarily essential for your supervisor to have particular expertise in the area you'll be investigating, it is preferable and can lead to more productive supervisions. A supervisor who is familiar with the area will be able to orientate themselves more quickly to issues and questions raised by you and your study and locate them more easily within the broader context of the discipline. It is also more likely that they will have an inherent interest in your research and therefore be more eager to see it conducted well and brought to a successful conclusion. This in turn may lead to them giving you more of their time!

- *Will their personal views be too overpowering?*
Although it is generally desirable for a supervisor to have expertise in your particular area of inquiry, there can also be certain risks. They may well have very strong views on the subject, leading to their students feeling pressured into adopting similar perspectives to themselves and skewing their research accordingly. In this respect, a supervisor's job is a very responsible and quite difficult one. They have to try to guide their students and encourage them to think creatively and independently, while remaining fairly neutral themselves. This can be a difficult balance to strike and you have to judge as best you can whether a potential supervisor is up to the task. It can be helpful if you already know them and have worked or studied with them, and asking colleagues or other students who have been or are being supervised by them can be very informative. Experience can also be important. An experienced supervisor is perhaps less likely to fall into this trap, even though his or her own views may have become fairly entrenched over the years!

- *Is their personality compatible with my own?*
Your supervisor is a key figure in the research process; somebody who you will meet regularly and whose job it is to guide you, act as a sounding board for your ideas, and keep you motivated during periods where your project may feel like it's floundering. Over time, and especially in the case of longer research projects, a supervisor can become a friend, someone you can depend on, and probably the only person who really knows what it is you are doing and who understands the highs and lows you will almost certainly experience. Clearly, then, if they are to fulfil this role effectively, you will need to get along with each other. In an ideal world, they will get excited by what you are doing and enjoy being involved, and you will benefit from their knowledge and experience. While you do not necessarily need to become the best of friends, there should be a mutual respect and, hopefully, plenty of humorous moments along the way. Unfortunately, as in any area of life, personalities sometimes clash and/or your supervisor may be unable to provide you with the particular kind of support you as an individual need. Sometimes these difficulties can be worked out over time, but occasionally there is nothing else for it but to request a change of supervisor, where possible. You should not be afraid to take this option if

you feel it necessary; after all, it is your project and your time and money that are being invested.

- *Will they be available to supervise me when I need guidance?*
  In choosing a supervisor, beware of high-profile academics. Those with worldwide reputations are always in high demand and often over-stretched; this means they are frequently absent from their department and unavailable for consultations as a result of overseas travel, conference presentations, commitments to other institutions and so on. Finally, it can also mean that they are so bound up in their own research that they are unable to devote adequate time to their research students. However, it is also true that high-profile academics can be the most exciting and inspiring to work with, and the richness of their experience can make supervisions memorable events. You will need to judge, therefore, whether this trade-off is acceptable to you. If, for example, your personality and project is such that you are able to work more independently, then the advantages of an exceptional academic and supervisor who has only limited availability may well outweigh the disadvantages. If, however, you feel you need more intensive guidance and support, you may want to look elsewhere. While it is possible to make inquiries and take advice about different supervisors' styles and availability, only you can make the final decision.

Your supervisor's role, then, is to act as a guide, and possibly as a mentor, but not to lead you to where they think you ought to go. Whether undergraduate or postgraduate, your research should be independent and your supervisor must try to strike a balance between keeping you on the straight and narrow while allowing you the freedom to develop your project in the way you see fit. They should alert you to pitfalls and play devil's advocate by acting as a sounding board, but not control your research. They should help you identify potentially productive lines of inquiry, source relevant literature and related projects (completed or in progress) and even put you in touch with useful individuals and/or institutions, where this may be beneficial. Finally, they should give you encouragement and help you through any lows you may experience during the course of your project. And to do these things most effectively, they need to be approachable, comfortable to work with and available. If you do have to compromise on one or more of these things, be sure that you can live with that compromise.

5.6 Writing a proposal

Before commencing with your research, you will be asked to submit a proposal describing the nature of your project and the motivation for it, and giving an indication of how you intend to conduct it. This proposal is normally no more than two sides of A4 in length and serves two important purposes. First, it forces you, the researcher, to clarify your own thinking. Often, it is only when we have to explain our thinking to others that we realize our ideas are only half-cooked, and if *we* are not clear about what it is we are doing, then *others* will certainly not be clear either. Second, a proposal gives the department an opportunity to judge whether the project is viable and whether you as a researcher have thought it through adequately and are capable of bringing it to fruition. A proposal also allows them to decide whether they have a specialist in the department qualified and willing to supervise the project.

The format of a proposal is fairly standard and needs to contain the following elements:

- *Title and subject*: the department needs to see a working title of the project, one that is concise and gives a clear indication of its focus.
- *The context of the project*: provide some information on what motivated your research idea and how it fits into the field and current thinking. Show you are familiar with the relevant literature on the subject – its history, key theories, articles, debates and so on – and keep your language clear and simple.
- *Statement of aims and objectives*: this section should explain what your research is designed to achieve, what problem it seeks to address, and the nature of the key constructs pertinent to solving that problem. For example, if your objective is to establish whether private schools are more successful than state schools, your main construct will be *success*. Those indicators of success which can be measured are called *variables* – examination results for instance – and you need to explain the role these will play in your study. The statement of aims and objectives only needs to be brief and should follow naturally from your discussion of the project's context. Remember: state clearly and precisely what the exact focus of your research is by identifying and listing your main research questions and discussing briefly those variables that will shed light on the main construct(s) involved. As we shall see later, while variables can help you as a researcher gain insight into the key constructs underpinning your research question(s), they can also muddy the waters in certain cases and make life quite difficult. The solution lies in the careful and creative design of your methodology.
- *Formulating your hypotheses*: Next, in light of your objectives, you will need to formulate a set of hypotheses. These are simply statements – expressed as assertions – about the anticipated outcomes of your study, and as such they indicate the different ways that you, the researcher, expect the study to turn out. They are typically phrased as follows:

To meet these objectives, I will test the following hypotheses:

1. *The number of A/A* grades achieved at GCSE level will be consistently higher in private schools than in state schools.*

2. *The number of A grades achieved at A-Level will be consistently higher in private schools than state schools.*
3. *The proportion of students successfully gaining entry to a university of their choice will be higher for private schools than for state schools.*

- *An indication of your methodology*: having contextualized your study and established your aims and objectives, you will need to explain how you plan to achieve those aims and objectives; in other words, what methods you plan to use. Different parts of your project may require different methods of data collection and analysis and so you will need to become familiar with these and explain which methods you have used for what purposes and why. Equally, you may wish to state why you have chosen *not* to use certain methods.
- *Expected outcomes*: although it would be foolish to make absolute predictions about research that has yet to be undertaken, you may well have expectations about the eventual findings of the project. Spell these out, being careful to justify them and not to exaggerate them.
- *A time frame for completion*: spell out how long you expect your project to take. This information is helpful to your potential supervisor for it indicates that you have planned out the project. It also has the advantage of forcing you to think ahead and organize your research, and of establishing milestones which can help motivate you and maintain momentum – even if you are ultimately unable to maintain the schedule.

Of course, as all researchers and supervisors know and expect, many of these details will change once your research begins and develops. What is important at this stage is the need to show yourself and your department/supervisor that you have a viable project, along with the tools and know-how to conduct it effectively and bring it to a successful conclusion.

In the case of undergraduate research, there tends to be more flexibility and less formality over dissertation proposals, although the key elements should still be present, as should a clear statement of what it is the project sets out to achieve and how – after all, this is good practice regardless of the level at which you are conducting your research. Furthermore, it is increasingly common at undergraduate level as well as postgraduate level for students to be asked to present their proposed projects to their peers, research groups and so on, as a way of clarifying their own thinking and benefiting from the feedback of their audience.

5.7 Adopting the correct mindset

Having written your proposal and had it accepted, you should be clear about precisely what you are doing in your research, what you hope to achieve, and how you intend to achieve it. Even though your project may well change shape over time, this principle of clarity and forethought must inform every stage of your research and the reporting of it. It must become part of your mindset and form background to everything you do if you are not to lose your way.

Similarly, analysis and critical evaluation will need to become second nature to you. By adopting a critical fame of mind, you maintain control of what you are doing by learning from others' mistakes and anticipating, identifying and avoiding problems before they seriously undermine your research and attract the criticism of examiners and peers.

Finally, when reporting your research you must always keep the reader at the forefront of your mind. Try to see your work from their perspective and continually ask yourself whether what you are writing is transparent and well argued.

5.8 Studying independently

It is often said that doing research can be a very lonely business. Most of the time you will probably be working alone, and there will be nobody looking over your shoulder making sure that you are getting on with it, although your supervisor may give you a prod from time to time! What's more, you may have to fit your research into a busy life that includes family, work, social and other commitments. This means that you will need to be organized, systematic and disciplined; in other words, efficient. In order to maximise the time you have available, we would recommend the following:

- *Organize your study area*: although everybody has a different way of working, most people feel calmer and more positive and in control working in a tidy environment, one in which they know where everything is.
- *Careful time management*: decide which days or parts of your days you are going to devote to your research, and try your best to stick to your time-table. As far as possible, arrange it so that you are working at those times of the day when you feel brightest and there are fewest disturbances, and be sure to build in short breaks when you switch off completely and recharge your batteries. Remember, although you may feel as though you are wasting time, brief periods of rest actually increase productivity and will help you keep going longer. Check when college or university facilities, such as the library and canteen, are open and take account of this information when creating your timetable.

- *Take a library tour*: this can be invaluable if you are unfamiliar with your library. Not only will it introduce you to the systems and services that are available to help you with your research, it will also save you time later by familiarizing you with the layout of the library. In particular, it will help you identify where the books, journals, dissertations and theses relevant to your own discipline and projects are located.
- *Try to set clear and manageable goals or milestones*: having something to aim at helps to maintain momentum and ensure progress. It also gives you a sense of achievement, which in turn will help keep you motivated.
- *Record information methodically*: it's all too easy to let your desire to 'get on with it' overcome the need to note down your sources. Even if it sometimes means interrupting your flow, make sure that you're in a position later on (sometimes *much* later on) to link information to its correct source easily. Failure to keep clear records can result in enormous frustration and costly delays further down the line. It's a good idea to develop a personal filing system, either electronic or consisting of index cards. While index cards may feel like a relic from the pre-IT age, they have the advantage of being available to you when there's a power cut, or worse, your computer hard drive crashes . . . permanently! Don't forget, frequently back up any work you have stored electronically and try to get in the habit of saving your work at the end of every two or three sentences.
- *Don't get bogged down in detail*: although there are times when it's important to look at the detail, doing so can sometimes be an obstacle to clear thinking and can leave you confused, disorientated and unable to see the wood from the trees. It is often necessary to 'step back' a little, to see the broader picture and to think in terms of general principles. Too great a concern with detail can also act as a distraction, causing you to digress from the more central and important issue(s).
- *Discuss ideas with colleagues (where appropriate)*: this can be a good way of getting you to think further about your ideas and can sometimes help you decide whether to pursue them or discard them. Often, bouncing ideas off other people can trigger insights of your own and get you thinking about things in a way or from a perspective you hadn't considered before. Some people are understandably cautious about discussing aspects of their research – and in particular any original ideas – with other people in case those people decide themselves to pursue and develop them. You will need to decide which ideas, if any, you are happy to discuss and whether there is any risk of them being appropriated and used in other research projects or as the subject of academic articles.
- *Develop your professional vocabulary*: try to become so familiar with the language and vocabulary of your field that its use becomes second nature to you. Every field, and even the sub-fields within it, has its own discourse, its own way of talking about the subject, and you need to be able to develop a natural fluency in the discourse of your own subject. If, for example, you hear two 'insiders' discussing, say, stocks and shares or the currency

markets, they have a language all their own and are perfectly comfortable in their use of it. They are able to 'talk' to each other in a way that we probably could not. You need to achieve the same in your particular research field.

5.9 Attending research seminars, conferences etc.

As we've seen, attending research seminars and conferences is one way of generating ideas for possible research projects; in fact, just as journal articles will often suggest proposals for further research, it is common for presenters to highlight the need for a certain kind of research or to simply trigger ideas in their audiences. However, attending these events may also provide ideas of ways you can develop and refine a research project you already have underway.

5.10 Understanding disciplinary differences

Although there are general principles governing how to conduct and write up research, you need to be aware that there are also particular elements which may be discipline specific, particularly with regard to the formatting of your research report. It is important that you familiarize yourself with these early on. Often, by the time they come to conducting research themselves, students are already quite well versed in the style normally adopted in their own field; they learn it largely through reading the work of other authors and researchers. However, being familiar with it is different from *noticing* it, understanding its significance and actually internalizing particular stylistic and formatting conventions so that you are able to use them productively. It can be helpful, therefore, to refer to style guides that are frequently produced by individual academic departments or university Information Services. And, of course, you can always take advice from your supervisor and other lecturers and fellow-students in the department.

5.11 The upgrading process (PhDs only)

If you are working on a PhD research project, it may well be that you are required initially to register as an MPhil student. You can view this as a kind of probationary period during which you will need to show the department that you are capable of doing research of the quality necessary to obtaining a PhD degree. Usually you will upgrade one or two years into your project, although the timing is largely up to you. In order to upgrade, you will need to produce a table of contents for your thesis, along with some sample chapters and possibly some commentary. The procedure is internal, so a qualified academic within the department will look at these materials and then meet with you – and probably your supervisor – to question you about the project and to comment on your work and the direction you are taking with it. This can be a very helpful process as it is an opportunity for someone not directly involved with the project to bring a fresh perspective to it. Often the comments that come out of the interview feed into the project and help to improve it. These comments are recorded in a formal report. If the interview goes well and the department is satisfied that your research is on track, has a good chance of reaching a successful conclusion and is of the required standard, then you will be upgraded and registered as a full PhD student.

5.12 Familiarity with 'Codes of Practice'/Rules and Regulations

Although you don't really need to worry early on about most of the rules and regulations that apply to the conducting of research, the writing and submission of your report and the procedures that you are required to go through, it is nevertheless a good idea to have some knowledge of these from day one. All universities publish a small booklet of rules and regulations for students pursuing research degrees, and a cursory glance through this should suffice and enable you to spot the key points you need to be aware of and to avoid any nasty shocks later on!

5.13 Ethical considerations

Conducting research frequently requires sensitivity to the effects of your research methods on those around you – particularly your subjects. This is especially true of the science and social science disciplines, which often involve working with people or animals and collecting data through interviews, questionnaires or laboratory experiments. As a researcher, you need to consider the possible moral dimensions of what you are doing: whether your behaviour could be detrimental in any way to your subjects; whether you are being honest and open with them and if not, whether your research really depends on a lack of openness and whether the potential benefits of the research justify it. Also consider whether your methodology and the motivation for it could be misconstrued and/or legal action be taken against you. If you think you might be skating on thin ice and feel that your research could lead to problems, take advice, and do so as quickly as possible. Don't wait until the project is well underway; try to anticipate possible difficulties at the design stage so that you don't waste months on a methodology that is undermined by ethical problems. Following are a few tips on how you can avoid such problems:

- *Make sure your subjects are well informed*: explain your methods, the reasons behind what you are doing and the use to which you will put the information they give you. Apart from anything else, people usually feel less intimidated and more inclined to participate – and to do so wholeheartedly – if they understand what they are contributing to, how and why. Equally, if you're unable to share with them the object of the data collection exercise without defeating its purpose, then try to explain this. You can (a) offer to share this information with them once the data has been collected and (b) agree not to use the data if, at that point, the subject is uncomfortable with your doing so.
- *Ask your subjects' permission*: put simply, allow them the chance to decline the opportunity to contribute to your research by asking them *very explicitly* whether they are happy to take part. It's best to avoid cajoling those who are clearly uncomfortable with doing so as this could lead to trouble later. In cases where the information you are requesting is particularly sensitive, you may wish to formalize your subjects' participation via a signed agreement in which you state the nature of the research and the data collection exercise and the willingness of the subject to take part. If, for purposes of the experiment and the integrity of the data collected, certain information needs to be withheld, then you might include a clause to that effect and saying that the subject has agreed to participate under those conditions.
- *Protect your subjects' privacy*: it is usually unnecessary to refer to subjects by name as the data itself, rather than who provides it, is often the key and the main focus of attention. However, if you do need to refer to particular subjects, you should not use their real names; use pseudonyms instead. This helps ensure that the subjects feel relaxed about providing information, especially when it's of a personal nature.
- *Share your recorded data and the results of your research*: it can be a good idea to show your records of interviews and so on to the subjects themselves before committing them to paper. This not only gives them a final opportunity to confirm that they are happy for you to go ahead and use the data they have provided, it also allows you the opportunity to check your own understanding or interpretation of what was said. Similarly, offering to share the final results of your research with contributors (whether subjects of not) is part of what we might call research etiquette!

- *Be courteous*: showing recorded data and the results of your research to contributors is a courtesy on your part as a researcher in payment for their time,
  effort and trust in helping make your project a success. But so too is being
  punctual, organized and to the point so that you inconvenience them as
  little as possible while efficiently and effectively collecting the data you
  need. Be sensitive where necessary and avoid accidentally causing offence.
  And, of course, always remember to thank them for their help; after all, your
  first attempt at data collection may prove to be flawed and you may need to
  return for more!
- *Always strive to be honest and objective*: this is something that we will look at
  later on. For the moment, however, let's just say that being honest and
  objective isn't as straightforward as you might think. It can be tempting to
  read into your data what you want to find there and it is therefore important to continually question your own integrity and objectivity. As with
  astrology and star signs, people are naturally disposed to interpret things in
  a way that fits with their experience, expectation and hopes!

5.14 The importance of finding your own 'voice' . . . and why it can be challenging

People often talk about the need for research students to 'find their own voice'
and to express that voice in their writing. Let's briefly look at what this means,
why it's considered important, and how you can find *your* own voice.

Finding your own voice really means two things. First, it means developing
your own distinctive style of writing, your own way of expressing what it is
you want to say; and this, of course, is something all writers try to achieve
whether they are journalists, novelists or academics. However, in the context
of conducting and writing up your research, this expression takes on added
significance. In particular, it refers to the need for you, as a researcher, to
formulate your own opinions, to adopt a critical stance; in other words, to take
a view on things and to have your own particular perspective. Whether your
research is empirically based or library based, it is not sufficient simply to
present or repeat facts and data generated by your research or sourced from the
literature; you need to analyse the information, establish whether or not it is
soundly based, and comment on it in a way that adds clarity and insight. You
may remember from our introduction that handbooks of Academic Regulations for Research Degrees talk about 'the exercise of independent critical
power'; it is precisely the written expression of this which helps you create
your own voice.

When writing in an academic context, it can often be difficult to strike a
balance between expressing your own viewpoint and showing an awareness of
and acknowledging the views of other, often well established and respected

writers. It is easy to feel overawed and to believe that you are not good enough or that you have nothing worthwhile to say, and you may therefore be understandably cautious about diverging from the views of authority figures and taking your own stand on issues. Unfortunately, such caution can result in writing that is boring, unimaginative and unoriginal because it ends up doing little more than describing the work of others. However, as we have seen, for a researcher attempting to break new ground, confidence and sure-footedness are crucial. Such confidence comes from having a good grasp of the relevant literature on the subject with which you are engaged, being clear about your own views on issues (you need to know what you believe before you express it and create your own voice), and knowing that your own project is well designed and methodologically sound (see Section 6.8). It is also a product of training and practice in critical appraisal and good argument. And be careful: confidence which comes from deep knowledge and understanding is not the same thing as arrogance, blinkeredness and reckless dogmatism – qualities that will seriously undermine your research and the way in which it is received by your peers, supervisor and examiner(s).

Striking a balance between acknowledging the views of established and respected writers and expressing your own viewpoint is essentially a process of negotiation between the need to 'doff your cap' to the conventions of university writing and to work within the framework of what is already known and understood, while also pushing the barriers and having your own say in your own way. It is only by working within the constraints imposed by the need to do the former that any efforts to inject yourself into your writing via the latter will be accepted and respected. But remember, establishing your own voice does not mean losing objectivity in your discussion and analysis. Your views must always be well informed and remain balanced and unbiased if they are to be taken seriously. It is perfectly possible to maintain objectivity while also retaining a sense of ownership and authority in your writing.

This need to establish your own voice is something with which students new to higher education and/or coming from other education systems overseas can sometimes struggle. Undergraduate students, in particular, sometimes enter higher education having been spoon-fed during secondary school, where the main emphasis may have been on storing and correctly reproducing information rather than on critically 'debating' ideas, taking a stand and expressing their own views. Furthermore, they may not be practised at researching information, organizing and noting it down, amplifying on ideas and broadening a focus of inquiry. All of these things can make for a difficult transition and leave students initially feeling insecure and uncertain, particularly when embarking on dissertations for the first time. This can be equally true of some postgraduate students or mature students who are returning to education after an extended period away from it.

In the case of international students, other challenges may present themselves. For those who come from very hierarchical cultures and/or cultures underpinned by philosophies which hold teachers and educators in high regard or consider outspokenness (particularly among peers) to be inappropriate, it can be extremely difficult – and counter-instinctive – to adopt and express a personal and critical voice. This can be especially true of certain Middle Eastern and Far Eastern cultures, where students often feel unable to question the authority of professors and published academics, regardless of whether they are writing an assignment, a dissertation or a thesis. And, of course, there is the personality factor too: some students are naturally shy and self-deprecating, and feel uncomfortable expressing a view – particularly a strong view – either in writing or verbally. While most lecturers are generally sensitive to these things and sympathetic, it is important, nevertheless, to try and overcome any such inclinations and to fully engage in the process of critically appraising ideas, if your work is to be an engaging, stimulating and provocative.

5.15 Getting down to writing

Eventually, of course, you will face the quite daunting task of recording all aspects of your project in detail, from its initial conception to the final conclusions you have been able to draw from your results and analysis. And it is to this important task that we now turn. If you would like further information on the more general issues surrounding the formulation and conducting of research projects, you may find the following sources helpful:

- *How to Get a Ph.D.* (Phillips and Pugh);
- *The Research Student's Guide to Success* (Cryer);
- The Open University Press study skills website: http://www.openup.co.uk/studyskills.

6

What are the different components of a research project?

6.1 Title page • 6.2 Abstract • 6.3 Acknowledgements • 6.4 List of contents • 6.5 List of acronyms and abbreviations • 6.6 Introduction • 6.7 Literature review • 6.8 Methodology • 6.9 Results/data • 6.10 Analysis and discussion • 6.11 Conclusions • 6.12 Bibliography • 6.13 Appendices

A dissertation or thesis will typically contain the following sections in the order they are listed:

- *Preliminary sections*: Title page
  Abstract
  Acknowledgements
  List of contents
  List of tables, figures and illustrations
- *Body of the work*: Introduction
  Literature review
  Main body/descriptive section
  Results (if the research is empirically-based)
  Discussion
  Conclusion
- *Supporting sections*: Bibliography
  Appendices

Each of these sections will now be discussed in more detail.

6.1 Title page

The title page of a research report should not be numbered. The pages of all other preliminary sections, however, should be numbered using Roman numerals, with the page immediately following the title page being numbered as 'ii'. The pages of the main body of the text are normally numbered with Arabic numerals (1, 2, 3 . . .).

The title of your report needs to indicate the nature and purpose of your research. It should be brief and to the point, and contain the key words or concepts underlying the work. Below are two examples of thesis titles:

The Effects of Hillslope-Channel Coupling on Catchment Hydrological Response in Mediterranean Areas

The Politics of Council Housing Decline: Divergent Responses in Rural England in the 1980s

---

Following are two reduced-size examples of thesis title pages designed to illustrate two types of layout traditionally used:

IMMIGRATION AND SOCIAL COHESION IN CONTEMPORARY BRITAIN: AN ASSESSMENT OF GOVERNMENT STRATEGY FROM 1945 - 2000

Martina Lopez

2004

King's College London University of London

A thesis submitted to the University of London for the degree of Doctor of Philosophy

The copyright of this thesis rests with the author and no quotation from it or information derived from it may be published without prior written consent of the author

---

What Makes One Speaker 'Better' than Another: An Inquiry into the Judgement Process in Foreign Language Oral Proficiency Assessment

by

Neil L. Murray

A Dissertation Submitted In Partial Fulfilment of The Requirements for the Degree of

M.PHIL IN ENGLISH AND APPLIED LINGUISTICS

Research Centre for English and Applied Linguistics University of Cambridge August 1992

Normally, if there is a colon in the title, whatever follows the colon begins on a new line (as in both the previous examples).

6.2 Abstract

Your abstract should be a summary of the essential elements of your research project. It should serve as an overview, providing the reader with a good indication of what he or she will find in the pages that follow. This is important because the abstract is the most read part of any research report, for it is frequently on the basis of the abstract that people decide whether or not the report is relevant to their own research (or other) interests and therefore worth reading. Typically, abstracts are between 250 and 300 words in length and should not go beyond one side of A4. An abstract will normally include:

- a statement of the main question or problem (i.e. the purpose of the research);
- the method(s) used to address it;
- the results obtained;
- the conclusions reached.

Sometimes the author may also give a brief account of any recommendations for future research made in the thesis and which derive from the research and its findings as documented in the thesis (see also Section 6.11).

TASK 1

Look at the following abstract. Try to identify the four features of abstracts already listed.

This research aims specifically to examine the sensitivity and response of shallow landslide hydrology to climate change and vegetation using hydrological modelling techniques. A one-dimensional tank model is used to investigate the sensitivity of shallow landslide hydrology to soil and vegetation parameters; and water table response to long-term rainfall and temperature variation. A three-dimensional version of the model is then used to assess the effect of the vegetation cover on water table distribution. Processes represented by the models include canopy interception, evapotranspiration, infiltration, macro-pore flow, and saturated and unsaturated movement of ground water.

The models were parameterized, calibrated and validated for two field sites situated in landslide-prone peripheral farming areas. This allowed a comparison of the effect of five different vegetation types within each environment. While the Roughs escarpment (SE England) is characterised by clay soils and weak clays that overlay a more impervious Weald clay, the gullied terraces of the Planes de Baronia basin (SE Spain) consist of predominantly silty-clayey soils over marl bedrock. In both environments, instability is caused by a rising water table. This study improves upon previous work at each site by describing the hydrologic significance of vegetation within long-term climate scenarios, and assessing the sensitivity of the landslides to variation in soil properties and rainfall characteristics.

Results of modelling indicate that projected changes in climate will have a greater impact at the site in SE Spain due to greater increases in mean winter rainfall. Though reflected in a relatively small rise in mean annual water table height (up to 0.18 ± 0.003m within the next 60 years), the probability of slope instability was predicted to rise by over 100%, due to a concurrent increase in rainfall variability. In contrast, mean water table height at the site in SE England is predicted to decrease by 0.05m ± 0.001 within the next 60 years, as the projected increase in annual rainfall is mitigated by increased evapotranspiration. Indeed, the effect of vegetation on slope hydrology was found to be more significant than the effects of climate change at both sites. This supports the view that vegetation cover may be used to decrease the risk of landslides in areas adversely affected by expected climate change.

Because the nature and design of your research is quite likely to change over time, it is a good idea to leave the writing of the title and abstract until the final stages. This avoids wasting time and having to change it at a later stage in order to reflect any significant changes your research may have undergone.

   TASK KEY

TASK 1

This research aims specifically to examine the sensitivity and response of shallow landslide hydrology to climate change and vegetation using hydrological modelling techniques.[1] A one-dimensional tank model is used to investigate the sensitivity of shallow landslide hydrology to soil and vegetation parameters; and water table response to long-term rainfall and temperature variation. A three-dimensional version of the model is then used to assess the effect of the vegetation cover on water table distribution. Processes represented by the models include canopy interception, evapotranspiration, infiltration, macro-pore flow, and saturated and unsaturated movement of ground water.

The models were parameterized, calibrated and validated for two field sites situated in landslide-prone peripheral farming areas. This allowed a comparison of the effect of five different vegetation types within each environment.[2] While the Roughs escarpment (SE England) is characterized by clay soils and weak clays that overlay a more impervious Weald clay, the gullied terraces of the Planes de Baronia basin (SE Spain) consist of predominantly silty-clayey soils over marl bedrock. In both environments, instability is caused by a rising water table. This study improves upon previous work at each site by describing the hydrologic significance of vegetation within long-term climate scenarios, and assessing the sensitivity of the landslides to variation in soil properties and rainfall characteristics.

Results of modelling indicate that projected changes in climate will have a greater impact at the site in SE Spain due to greater increases in mean winter rainfall. Though reflected in a relatively small rise in mean annual water table height (up to 0.18 ± 0.003m within the next 60 years), the probability of slope instability is predicted to rise by over 100%, due to a concurrent increase in rainfall variability. In contrast, mean water table height at the site in SE England is predicted to decrease by 0.05m ± 0.001 within the next 60 years, as the projected increase in annual rainfall is mitigated by increased evapotranspiration.[3] Indeed, the effect of vegetation on slope hydrology was found to be more significant than the effects of climate change at both sites. This supports the view that vegetation cover may be used to decrease the risk of landslides in areas adversely affected by expected climate change.[4]

[1] = a statement of the main question or problem (i.e. the purpose of the research)
[2] = the method(s) used to address it
[3] = the results obtained
[4] = the conclusions reached

6.3 Acknowledgements

The acknowledgements section is where you as the researcher and writer of the report thank those individuals and institutions that have assisted with or contributed to your research in some way. This may be through the provision of funding, facilities, services or data, or less directly via discussion and consultation, advice, motivation, and simply empathy and friendship during what can be a challenging time in your academic career. The one person who will almost certainly feature in the acknowledgements is your supervisor! It is considered a matter of courtesy to recognize these people and institutions . . . and to spell their names correctly!

Look at the following sample 'Acknowledgements' page.

ACKNOWLEDGEMENTS

This thesis would not have been possible without the generous support of the Rothermere Foundation. In 1986, I received the Rothermere Foundation Fellowship, which is awarded yearly to a graduate student of Memorial University. The Fellowship permits the recipient to study at any institution in the United Kingdom, and has supported many distinguished scholars in the years since it was first instituted in 1956 by Viscount Rothermere who was then the Chancellor of Memorial University.

At the time of my application, I was fortunate to come to the attention of Dr Deirdre Wilson, who agreed to act as my supervisor. In the years during which this research has wound its leisurely way to a conclusion, she has provided guidance, support, understanding and professional and personal assistance of the most valuable kind. Through Dr Wilson I learned about relevance theory; and whatever contribution to relevance theory may be represented by this thesis, I have discovered in the theory itself the key to questions raised by my experiences as a student and teacher of literature – questions which had never been satisfactorily addressed before. For this alone I am immensely grateful.

I wish also to acknowledge my gratitude to the Department of Linguistics at University College London for the patience, courtesy, and support I have unfailingly encountered in the long course of completing this work.

To Dr Abbas and Mrs Shomais Afnan, and to Ms Sahba Akhavan, I owe a considerable debt. Their openhearted hospitality allowed me to return to the United Kingdom and complete the work on and the writing of this thesis.

Dr Peter Baehr was kind enough to share his own work with me. For the opportunity to read 'Founders, Classics, and the Concept of a Canon' (Baehr and O'Brien 1994), and to discuss the connections between his research and my own, I am very grateful.

6.4 List of contents

It is important that your list of contents is detailed and reflects accurately the structure of the research report. It should be arranged according to chapter/section numbers, incorporating all headings and sub-headings as they appear in the text, along with the page numbers on which they start. In order to indicate the status of different sections of the text, it is common practice to use a decimal numbering system:

Note: See Part 3, Appendices, for a sample Table of Contents.

Tables, figures and illustrations are normally numbered consecutively throughout the research report, and completely independently of the decimal numbering system used elsewhere. They will therefore follow a simple 'Figure 1, Figure 2, Figure 3 . . .' pattern, regardless of where they appear in the report. In the list of contents, however, it is important to indicate the page number on which each table, figure or illustration appears.

6.5 List of acronyms and abbreviations

It is quite common to find a list of acronyms and abbreviations at the start of a research report, usually following the List of Contents. Not surprisingly, researchers will typically draw on many written sources during the course of their projects and will consequently find it necessary to make reference to these in their writing. For the sake of convenience, rather than repeatedly writing out in full the names of source materials it is quicker and easier to refer to those materials using shortened forms – acronyms and abbreviations. Although the meaning of each acronym and abbreviation should be made clear after its first mention in the main text of the report, it is normal practice to provide a key to the meanings of these shortened forms in the first pages of the report. This allows for quick and easy reference on the part of the reader. Following is a sample List of Acronyms and Abbreviations taken from a real thesis.

LIST OF ACRONYMS AND ABBREVIATIONS

A.P.M.S.P.	Australian-Pacific Mail Steam Packet Company
B. Hist.	Business History
B.R.P.M.	Brazil and River Plate Mail
C.O.	Colonial Office

C.O. 318 etc.	Colonial Office papers in Public Record Office
C.G.T.	Compagnie Générale Transatlantique
G.S.A.V.	Compañia Sud-America de Vapores
Ec.H.R.	Economic History Review
fo.(s)	Folio(s)
F.O.	Foreign Office
F.O. 6, 13, 61 etc.	Foreign Office papers in Public Record Office
Greenwich	National Maritime Museum
H.A.H.R.	Hispanic-American Historical Review
I.A.E.A.	Inter-American Economic Affairs
J.E.H.	Journal of Economic History
J.T.H.	Journal of Transport History
M.G.C.	Manchester Guardian Commercial
P.S.N.	Pacific Steam Navigation Company
Parl. Debates	Parliamentary (House of Commons) Debates
Parl. Papers (P.P.)	Parliamentary (House of Commons) Papers
P & O	Peninsula and Oriental Company
Post 29, Post 33 etc.	Post Office Archives
Public Dept.	Public Department (i.e. Official) Correspondence
R.M.S.P.	Royal Mail Steam Packet Company
S.A.J.	South American Journal
U.C.L.	University College London
W.I.C.C.	West India Committee Circular

6.6 Introduction

The general principles underlying the writing of introductions were discussed in Part 1 of this guide. Here we will look more specifically at what an introduction to a research report needs to achieve, and therefore what elements it will typically include. These are as follows:

- *The motivation for your research*: you need to explain *why* you decided to embark on your research project. As we have seen, your motivation could be an observation you have made directly during the course of your professional life, a 'knowledge gap' which you have noticed in the literature of your subject, or some other source of inspiration. The introduction, then, is that part of the report where you indicate the provenance of your research, put it in perspective and set the scene for what is to come in the pages that follow.
- *The nature of the investigation*: this is where you should define clearly the research questions you intend to address in your investigation, the key

constructs underpinning them, the variables that will be influential in your investigation, and a statement of your hypotheses (see Sections 1.6, 5.6 and 6.8).

• *A brief description of how you approached your research questions*: this component should be a concise account of how you carried out your investigation. It should serve as a preface to the main Methodology section (see below) and as such the level of detail included should not go beyond what is necessary to give the reader a broad but clear overview of the approach you adopted in addressing your research questions.

Of course, these different elements are all interconnected. For example, as part of your explanation of the motivation for or background to your research, you will almost certainly describe your research questions and the way in which they emerged. In other words, it was because you identified a problem or discovered an important area of inquiry, as yet unaddressed, that you decided to conduct your research, in the hope of providing clarification and new insight.

It is often the case that the motivation for a research project lies in the researcher's personal experience or observations 'in the field', and this leads him or her to investigate an issue further and ultimately to carry out formal research. As a result, part of the introduction may be anecdotal in nature. For example, a medical practitioner may have observed that under certain conditions his or her patients always behave in a particular kind of way; as a result s/he decides to investigate why this is the case. Likewise, a teacher may find that students in the classroom respond differently to the same teaching methodology; as a result s/he decides to try and find out whether there is any clearly identifiable and systematic reason why different individuals respond differently. In both these examples the two researchers would likely make reference in their introductions to their experience in the surgery and classroom respectively.

6.7 Literature review

6.7.1 Why have a literature review?

The literature review typically follows the introduction to your research report and its importance cannot be overestimated. It is where you present, in summary form, other work (books, articles, documents etc.) the content of which relates in some way to your own research. The purpose of the review is:

- To show where your study fits into the broader scheme of things; how it connects with the existing body of knowledge on the subject or on other related issues. In doing so, it also shows how your own research is original and promises to contribute to that pool of knowledge. In other words, along with the introduction, it helps to contextualize or 'position' your research by placing it within a broader framework. This also helps you to avoid reinventing the wheel by needlessly repeating the work (and mistakes) of others.
- To help you locate information that may be relevant to your own research.
- To increase and display your knowledge of the subject – to the examiners in particular – and to convince them and your peers of the need, relevance and importance of your research and the suitability of the methodology you have adopted. Presenting what has been researched and written on a subject is one way of showing what needs to be done. It can do this by indicating the inadequacies of previous studies, by building on the findings of previous studies by taking them a step further, by highlighting an area of inquiry as yet unaddressed or unrecognized, or simply by taking a completely different approach to a subject or problem. In doing so, it shows the significance and value of your own research.
- to identify seminal (key, influential) works in your area of study.
- to identify methods, approaches and techniques that could be relevant to your own research.
- to familiarize yourself with different and/or opposing views and to demonstrate your ability to critique and evaluate the work of other scholars.

 The literature review should not be merely a list of relevant research works in the field, in chronological order, with a brief description of each. Instead it should include an overview of significant research related to your topic area, which you then evaluate in order to show the contribution of each and to point out any shortcomings.

6.7.2 Organizing the literature search

To ensure that you are familiar with the relevant work of scholars in your field, you will need to do a literature search. This can seem a daunting task as there may be a very large body of published material. Your supervisor will be able to offer advice on the best way to approach the task, but here are a few tips to help guide you:

- Conduct a search for a limited number of key books and journal articles on your topic published over the last few years. (Remember that many journals are now available on-line.)
- As you read the articles, summarize the main points (see Section 4.4, Recording Information/Making Notes).
- Do not check *only* books and articles that are directly relevant to your own research. Work that may seem a little peripheral to your own research topic can often include information that is very relevant or which triggers new ideas or directions of thought.
- As you move backwards chronologically through the literature be sure to check out any sources widely cited by authors you have read and which appear relevant to your own research.
- As you read, try to organize the literature according to its importance or relevance to your topic area.

6.7.3 Structuring the literature review

We have seen that the literature review is not simply a chronological list of previously published work. It plays an important role in creating a structure or framework that will allow you to display not only your *knowledge* of the relevant literature, but also your ability to summarize and critique the information and ideas it contains coherently. You can demonstrate this ability by:

- grouping texts (articles, chapters, books etc.) according to the similarity of their ideas or arguments,
- grouping studies that focus on similar phenomena or share similar methodologies;
- commenting on the main ideas that feature in each group of texts or studies, rather than simply quoting or paraphrasing them;
- comparing and contrasting the different studies, viewpoints, methodologies and so on, and identifying for the reader those which have the greatest bearing on your own research;
- indicating which articles, ideas, methodologies and so on will form the basis of your investigations.

Some of the most important citations are those referring to articles in refereed journals and you should include these in your literature review. You should be very cautious about using internet sources as these are not peer reviewed and therefore do not carry the same weight.

Although the dangers of over-quoting were highlighted in Section 2.3 (Plagiarism), the very nature of the literature review section of your dissertation/thesis means that you will inevitably devote much of this section to presenting and discussing the works of other scholars. Therefore, provided your literature review does not consist solely of a 'list' of citations of other scholarship, you will not be penalized for this.

6.7.4 The language of critiquing

Something you should consider when writing any section of your report is variety: you should try to use a range of vocabulary and grammatical structures in order to avoid monotony. Because you will probably be referring to numerous authors and viewpoints in your literature review, you will need to find different ways of introducing the authors you cite. Some of these were discussed earlier in Section 2.3, however, the use of the active and passive forms warrants special mention here.

6.7.4.1 A note on the active and passive forms

Look at the following two examples. Although they share the same information content, their structures and the effects they have on the reader are different:

> Peters (1992) *discovered* that . . . (active)
> It *was discovered* by Peters (1992) that . . . (passive)

In the case of the active form, where the discoverer's name is placed at the beginning of the sentence, the discoverer himself is given more prominence. This is useful when you wish to emphasize the discoverer more than or as well as his discovery. However, if you wish to give more emphasis to the discovery (as opposed to the discoverer) you may choose to use the passive tense. The active is used more widely than the passive, partly because it is easier to read and often creates a feeling of greater fluency. Remember, as a general rule, whatever is placed at the beginning of a sentence or clause is given greater prominence and therefore receives greater emphasis.

6.8 Methodology

6.8.1 What is it and why is it important?

The methodology section of a research report describes how you conducted your study and the methods you used to collect and analyse the data. The term 'methodology' refers to the general approach taken to the research process, while 'methods' refers more specifically to the various ways in which data is collected and analysed. Regardless of the field in which you are conducting your research, the overall aim of the methodology section is the same: to provide the reader with an overview of the methods employed so that a judgement can be made as to how appropriate they are given the objectives of the research, and how valid the data is that they have generated.

The following guidance notes are not intended to provide a comprehensive description and discussion of the various research methodologies, tools and techniques, but to alert you to a number of key issues you will need to consider in deciding and presenting your research methodology. You should discuss the details of individual methods and their suitability for your particular research with your tutor or supervisor.

The methodology you choose to use will serve as the underpinnings for your entire study, so your selection of the most suitable methodology is crucial. If you make bad choices at this early stage, they will have a ripple effect throughout your research, weakening its integrity and leading to questionable findings. Remember: your research is only as valid (and therefore valuable) as the methodology upon which it is based. Of course, there are many other factors that can affect the overall validity of your research – for example, how effectively you apply your methodology and how logical the deductions are that you make from your data; nevertheless, a study that is sound at the conceptual level is of primary importance. Implementing a poorly conceived study is like building a house on sand rather than on a firm foundation: it will never be secure and will eventually fail and collapse, and all the time and effort put into constructing it will be wasted.

In this section, then, you should present your methodology and rationale accurately and completely, but also as concisely as possible. You should also mention those methodological tools you considered but did *not* employ (particularly if they were used in related studies) and give the reason(s) why you decided not to use them your particular study.

6.8.2 Choosing an approach

At a very broad level, it is possible to distinguish between purely theoretical or 'library-based' research and empirical research. Purely theoretical research tends to be less common and does not involve the collection of data through experimentation or fieldwork. Instead, it may, for example, identify a problem in the existing literature, discuss it, and possibly provide some kind of resolution. It may deconstruct certain concepts, models and so on with a view to offering clarification and/or further refinement, or possibly substituting them altogether with 'improved' alternatives. The heart of empirical research, in contrast, lies in the collection of data via experimentation or fieldwork, and its subsequent analysis. Both approaches share the common goal of providing new insights and, by doing so, enriching the field.

Take, for instance, the topic of Communicative Language Teaching, a currently popular and widespread approach to language teaching originating in the 1970s. A library-based research project might involve a critical review of Communicative Language Teaching, a deconstruction of the approach involving a survey of the relevant literature and a detailed analysis of its theoretical underpinnings with a view to seeing whether these are sound or whether they are ill-informed and contain inconsistencies and contradictions.

An empirically-based research project on Communicative Language Teaching might, in contrast, attempt to establish via interviews and fieldwork in the form of classroom observations whether and to what extent language classrooms claiming to be communicative truly embody communicative principles as articulated in seminal literature on the approach, and whether teachers really understand the approach they claim to be using.

6.8.2.1 Quantitative vs qualitative methodology

In the case of empirical research, approaches normally fall into one of two categories or 'paradigms': *quantitative* and *qualitative*. The approach you adopt will depend partly on the academic discipline within which you are working and partly on the nature of your particular research project and the research questions you are attempting to answer.

A quantitative study is one in which the data you collect and analyse involves the accurate measurement of phenomena and, often, the application of statistical analysis. It is essentially concerned with numbers and anything that is quantifiable (or measurable) and as such uses methods such as psychometrics, statistical modelling techniques, datasets and services, experimental design and statistical computing and methodology.

A qualitative approach, on the other hand, involves the collection of information and its analysis rather than the application of quantitative methods. As such it is less concerned with numbers and accurate measurement and more concerned with the depth of data. It will typically involve the collection of data via interviews, focus groups, participant observation, oral history and so on.

The first approach (quantitative) is sometimes considered more 'scientific' and tends to be associated with the natural sciences and engineering, where phenomena are observed and (more easily) measured. In contrast, the second approach (qualitative) is sometimes seen as less 'scientific' in that, although it may also involve measurement, the kind of precision and measurability associated with the natural sciences is often not possible in the humanities and social sciences, which tend by their very nature to be less exact and involve a more subjective interpretation of facts, ideas and observed phenomena. This means that there are fewer clear-cut findings or results and, consequently, qualitative research tends to be more widely used in the social science disciplines. Ultimately, however, it is the 'problem' you are attempting to address in your research and the associated hypotheses you have constructed that will largely determine – even dictate – the type of methodological approach you adopt. In other words, during the process of reaching a decision about this crucial aspect of your project, you will need to ask yourself questions such as:

- What is the nature of the problem and what are my research questions? How can I express these as hypotheses? (see Section 5.6)

- Which methodology (quantitative or qualitative) will best allow me to solve or shed light on this problem and address my research questions?
- Which will provide me with an effective tool for obtaining accurate and valid data and, where applicable, for testing my hypotheses?

In terms of language, one notable difference between a quantitative and a qualitative methodological approach is the voice used to report on the methods used. It is customary to use the passive voice when writing up a scientific Methods section; this signals a more objective approach where the focus is firmly on the methods rather than the author (e.g. 'each occurrence of the phenomenon was noted'). In a qualitative study, the active voice appears more frequently and the first person singular 'I' is, arguably, more permissible, indicating as it does a more interactive approach (more typically a feature of qualitative research) taken by you, the author, in dealing with the subject(s) of your study. (See Section 3.2 for more information on the use of 'I' in academic writing.)

Other more detailed methodological questions you will need to consider when planning your research include:

- What difficulties do I anticipate in carrying out my research? (e.g. What variables will need controlling?) (see Section 5.6)
- Which methods are most suited to and most commonly adopted in the kind of research I am undertaking?
- Which methods are the most reliable and promise to provide me with the kind of data I require?
- Which methods can work best in combination by acting as mutual checks and providing the most comprehensive coverage of the area/phenomenon under investigation?
- Which methods are most practical if I need to collect my data within a limited time frame?
- Which methods are going to subject me to the most/fewest constraints? (Being dependent on the availability and reliability of human subjects, for example, can present difficulties and be very frustrating and time consuming).
- Which methods are likely to require replication?
- Which methods are/are not ethically acceptable or could be considered 'grey areas'?

Where they report on similar kinds of studies to the one you are undertaking, sources cited in your literature review (see Sections 4.3 and 6.7) can sometimes be a useful indicator of suitable methods to adopt. Moreover, the list of references provided by these authors can in turn also help direct you to related research, and methods utilized, that may be of relevance to the design of your own study.

Remember, whatever the nature of your study, there is no such thing as a perfect methodology. Any methodology will have advantages and disadvantages and none will provide an ideal solution to all the problems your research may potentially throw up; therefore, what you will normally end up with is a 'best compromise' methodology. The trick is to obtain the best fit possible between the questions you wish to address in your research and the methodological 'tool kit' that will most effectively provide valid answers to those questions.

To sum up, your methodology section should contain the following:

- A statement of the broad nature of the data you are seeking to obtain (a detailed description of data actually obtained will emerge in your Results and Discussion sections – see Sections 6.9 and 6.10).
- A description and explanation of your choice of methodology.
- A description of how, when and where you obtained your data.
- A rationale for your choice of certain methods and your rejection of others.
- The method(s) employed for analysing data, along with your rationale.
- An indication of some of the shortcomings or problems encountered with the methodology and the ways in which you solved them or sought to work around them.
- Mention of ethical considerations (in the case of human or animal subjects) where appropriate, and how these were dealt with (see also Section 5.13).

Although you will want to make reference to tools such as questionnaires in the Methodology section, the documents themselves are generally placed in the 'Appendices' section (see Section 6.13) at the end of your research report, particularly if they are lengthy documents.

Finally, be sure to provide a detailed account of your methodology. Remember: the findings of a study are only as valid as the methodology used to produce them. Therefore, if readers are unable to evaluate your methodology, then equally they are unable also to evaluate the findings of your study and their significance. And without the ability to do that, the research effectively becomes meaningless because its very foundations remain uncertain.

> **TASK 1**
>
> Photocopy the methodology section of a dissertation or thesis (plus one journal article describing an empirical study) relating to your area of research. Then do the following:

a. Make a note in the margin of what is discussed in each paragraph.
b. Underline in pencil all the verbs used (except for infinitives). Decide whether they are (i) in the active or passive voice; (ii) in the present or past tense.
c. Underline, in different colours, those sentences and phrases which:
    (i)   introduce the methodology;
    (ii)   describe the technique(s) used;
    (iii) describe the materials used (if applicable);
    (iv)   justify the choice of methodology;
    (v)   highlight any possible shortcomings of the methodology (if applicable).
d. In what order do i–v above appear in the research reports you are examining?
e. Do the verb voices or tenses differ in any of the sections you have identified? If so, why do you think the writer has switched voices/tenses for a particular section?
f. Were there any factors restricting the methodology? If so, what were they?
g. Compare the procedures followed in the two reports:
    (i)   are they clearly described?
    (ii)   could you replicate this study based on the researcher's description of the procedure followed? If not, why not?

 Try to examine a number of 'Methodology' sections before you design your own research in order to compare the methodologies used. This will not only give you ideas about possible approaches you might adopt in your own research but will also help familiarise you with the language conventions used.

6.9 Results/data

Occasionally, the presentation of research results is incorporated into the 'Discussion' chapter of a thesis, which is then headed 'Results and Discussion'.

This will tend to happen where it is felt that the results are likely to raise immediate questions or concerns in the mind of the reader which can be more effectively dealt with within the immediate context of the presentation of the results themselves rather than later, where they may feel more dislocated. In a qualitative study, for example, it can sometimes be difficult to disentangle results from their analysis/interpretation, and having one section where you can deal with both simultaneously may therefore be preferable. In general, however, the 'Results' section presents the findings of your research together with brief comments, particularly where statistical analysis is involved. More extensive comments appear later in the 'Discussion' section. Consult your supervisor for advice as to the best format to use for your particular research report.

> If you decide to have two separate sections, be careful to organize your material so that there is a clear division between the two – do not fall into the trap of having too much analysis in the 'Results' section.

6.9.1 Styles of presentation

The way in which you present your data will depend in part on whether that data is qualitative or quantitative. Quantitative data is usually presented using figures set out in the form of tables, graphs, charts and diagrams. When you present information in this way, you must of course make reference to it in your text, adding commentary to highlight and explain key aspects of the data.

A qualitative study may also present statistical data and employ graphs, charts and so on, but other types of data will likely also feature in such studies – data which, for example, record people's behaviour, attitudes, beliefs and opinions. This kind of data will often lend itself more to a fuller description written in normal prose, with figures being used to support and clarify points made in the text, as opposed to the text merely explaining the data presented in figures, such as in a quantitative study. Any such description needs to be accurate, succinct and coherent (see Section 2.1).

> A good word-processing programme such as Microsoft Word will have tools that allow you to produce clear and (where appropriate) colourful charts, graphs and tables. These will normally come with a choice of pre-designed formats from which you can choose. Such programmes also have drawing and painting tools with which you can create your own diagrams.

When making reference to a table, figure, chart or diagram, the following expressions may be helpful:

> *The graph in Figure 2 illustrates this trend.*
> *As can be seen in the graph below (Figure 8), there was a clear correlation between . . . and . . .*
> *Figure 3 highlights this growth in income over the past decade.*
> *The results obtained are presented as a bar chart in Figure 15. They clearly indicate . . .*
> *The table in Figure 4 records . . .*
> *The chart in figure 7 indicates/suggests . . .*
> *The response times of subjects were recorded and plotted on a graph (see Figure 8).*
> *Over 70% of respondents showed greater improvement in health as a result of taking the drug on a regular basis, as indicated in Figure 24.*
> *As Figure 5 illustrates, observations over a 3-month period reinforced these initial perceptions.*
> *Subjects' responses to the questionnaire were carefully compiled and recorded in tablature form (Figure 16).*

6.9.2 Tables, charts, graphs and diagrams

6.9.2.1 Tables

Data presented in a table are arranged in columns and rows. A computer spreadsheet (such as Excel) uses this pattern. Tables can be an effective method of presenting small sets of data as long as the table is well designed – in other words, clearly laid out and easy to understand. Poorly designed tables can be confusing and act as barriers to comprehension. For example, a lack of standardization in spacing between items and the use of upper case (capital) letters for both headings and sub-headings can make a table look untidy and difficult to read. Once you have chosen a particular format for, say, a main heading (e.g. all upper case letters) use it for all the main headings and choose a different format for sub-headings (e.g. capitalize only the first letter of the first word unless you are using an official acronym, such as PAYE for 'Pay As You Earn').

Do not make the mistake of overloading your reader: if you have a lot of statistics to present, consider how you can divide them into two or more tables rather than using one long table. For example, if you are presenting various data relating to six different countries, each country could be presented in a separate table – unless you are comparing and contrasting, in which case you may opt to use a single table in order to highlight more effectively the similarities and differences between the countries. You should also try to order items logically within a table. If, for example, you are listing the GDP (Gross Domestic Product) of a series of nations, with a view to comparing them and looking for trends, it would be preferable to list those nations in numerical order according to GDP rather than alphabetically according to their names. Why? Because such an arrangement answers much better the purpose of the table, allowing as it does for easier comparison and identification of any trends.

Finally, do not forget to give your table a title – this should be as short as possible but also meaningful, accurately reflecting the content of the table. Titles tend to consist of definite and indefinite articles (the/a), adjectives, nouns and prepositions; verbs are often omitted. Figure 6.1 shows an example of a simple table.

Labour Productivity Levels in EU Countries Relative to the USA			
Country	1979–90	1990–5	1995–2001
France	103.9	104.3	101.6
Germany	100.3	92.7	82.7
Italy	90.8	91.1	78.9
UK	63.3	81.9	75.3
EU–27	84.6	88	80.3
USA	100	100	100

FIGURE 6.1 Example of a table.

6.9.2.2 Charts

Data presented in charts have an immediate visual impact upon the reader and can provide an at-a-glance idea of trends, quantities and proportions. Today, with the help of elegant computer programmes such as Excel, spreadsheet data arranged in tables can be converted into charts and graphs quickly and easily with just a few mouse clicks. There are two main types of chart: pie charts and bar charts. Let's look briefly at each of these types.

Pie Charts: Pie charts are useful for presenting percentage data, with each 'slice' or segment of the pie representing a certain percentage of the total pie. For example, a pie chart would be an effective way of presenting sources of energy in the United Kingdom, by indicating the proportion of energy each source (oil, gas, coal, nuclear) contributes to the total energy supply. In general, try to avoid including too many segments in a pie chart as this will make it look cluttered; it will also lose its visual impact because the distinction between the different segments will be less obvious. If you do choose to display a large amount of data using a pie chart, selecting different shades and colours can help maintain clarity. Remember to include a key explaining what each colour/pattern-coded segment represents.

 When creating a pie chart, imagine that your chart is a clock face – put the largest slice at 12 o'clock and move round clockwise with the other slices in descending order.

Example

The pie chart in Figure 6.2 provides information on population.

World's Ten Largest Countries in Terms of Population

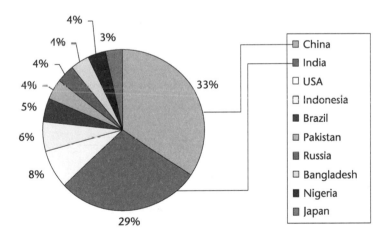

FIGURE 6.2 An example of a pie chart.

Bar charts: Bar charts should be used when making comparisons between two or more items. The data can be represented either by vertical bars (the most common type of bar chart, also referred to as a 'column' chart in some spreadsheet programmes) or horizontal bars. Because the length of each bar shows the value of the data, bar charts are a very effective way

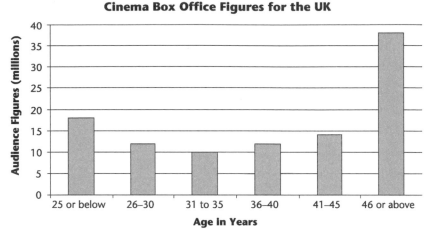

FIGURE 6.3 An example of a bar chart.

of presenting comparative data as the reader can see at a glance the similarities and differences between the items being compared. Figure 6.3 illustrates this, showing the different box office figures for different age groups in the United Kingdom.

Bar charts are also used to draw attention, in a single chart, to multiple features within a particular data set. Component bar charts, for example, can be used to show the proportions of a number of components or 'characteristics' within a particular item. Figure 6.4 is concerned with two items:

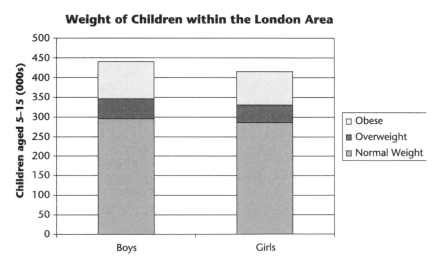

FIGURE 6.4 A further example of a bar chart.

male and female children. These are represented by two bars, one for each sex. As you can see, each of these two bars is divided into three components which indicate the number of children of each sex who are obese, overweight, or of normal weight.

Information can also be displayed using a multiple bar chart as in Figure 6.5.

Percentage of Working and Middle Class Students Entering Higher Education in the UK

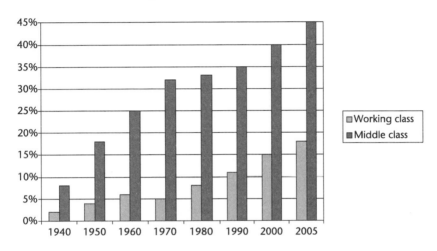

FIGURE 6.5 An example of a multiple bar chart.

More complex multiple bar charts can also be used to present information. Monthly sales figures over a one-year period could be presented as illustrated in Figure 6.6, for instance, with each bar representing the monetary value of products sold by each of three sales methods (A = internet sales, B = telephone sales, C = sales made through direct response to newspaper and magazine advertisements).

Finally, bar charts can be used to represent percentage data where two items are being compared (see Figure 6.7). This type of data is sometimes presented using horizontal bars with the percentages running along the *x*-axis and labels (figures or words) appearing on the *y*-axis. Horizontal bar charts are also useful when the labels (text) for each bar are too long to fit below vertical bars on the *x*-axis.

As with tables, charts should be given a title. Both tables and charts should also be numbered (e.g. 'Figure 3') for easy reference within the text. Colours, patterns and shading are also important: pie charts and multiple bar charts should be presented using a different pattern, colour or shade of grey for each segment or bar to make them clearly distinguishable.

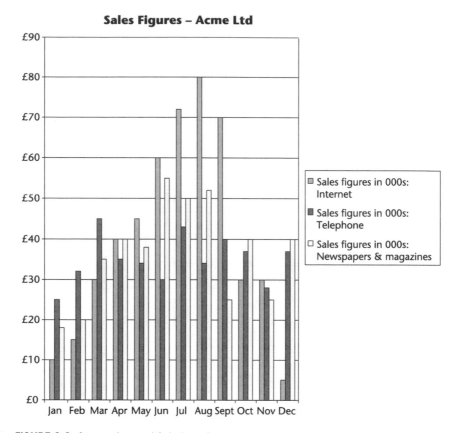

FIGURE 6.6 A complex multiple bar chart.

Histograms are similar in appearance to bar charts; however, histograms differ in that the area of the bars represents the frequency of an event. If a histogram has bars of the same width (i.e. the class intervals are equal) then the *heights of the bars* will indicate the frequency of the event. However, if the bars are of different widths (i.e. the class intervals are unequal) then the *area of the bars* will indicate the frequency of the event once the frequency density has been found and plotted on the vertical axis. Furthermore, in the case of histograms, the bars are placed side by side (with no spaces in between) to represent continuous data. This is illustrated in Figure 6.8.

6.9.2.3 Graphs

Line graphs are not suitable for discrete data. Instead, they are used to present continuous data spanning a particular time period. This can be useful, for

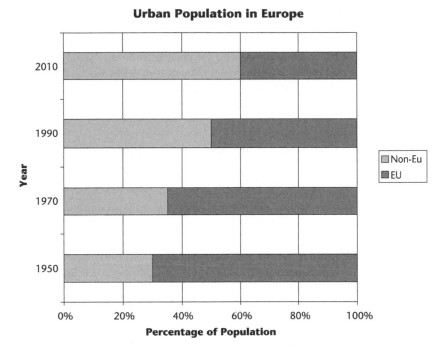

FIGURE 6.7 A bar chart representing percentage data.

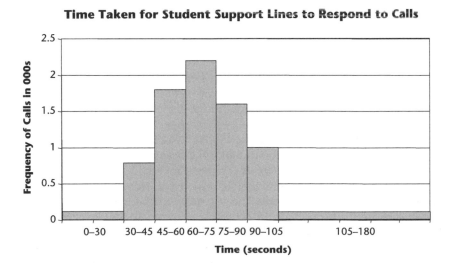

FIGURE 6.8 An example of a histogram.

example, when wishing to show the share price movements of a company over a period of weeks, months or years. Two or more parallel sets of data can also be presented in a line graph – for example, the sales figures for two divisions of the same company over the same period. In this case, in order to visually distinguish the two sets of data, each line is either colour-coded and/or employs different symbols for the points plotted on the graph, as in Figure 6.9.

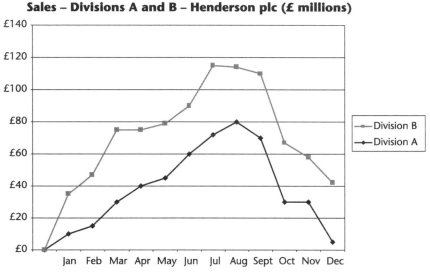

FIGURE 6.9 An example of a line graph.

Scatter graphs are used to show a causal link between two variables (*x* and *y*). The variable that is being influenced must be on the *y*-axis while the influencing variable is on the *x*-axis. If the points tend to cluster around a line running from lower left to upper right, there is a positive correlation (i.e. an increase in the value of one variable is accompanied by an increase in the other): for example, an increase in sales is associated with an increase in the number of sales staff or the number of hours people listen to the radio increases with age (Figure 6.10). If, on the other hand, the points cluster around a line running from upper left to lower right, the correlation is negative. This occurs if an increase in the value of one variable is associated with a decrease in the value of the other: for example, higher taxation may be associated with lower spending or, as in Figure 6.11, sales of hot beverages decline as summer temperatures increase. If the points on the graph are randomly distributed, this indicates that there is no correlation between the two variables.

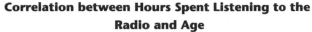

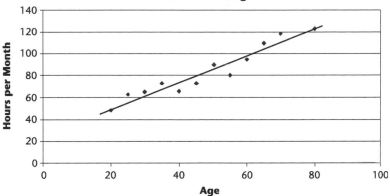

FIGURE 6.10 An example of a scatter graph.

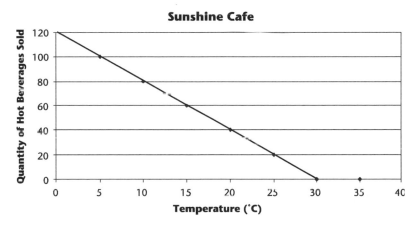

FIGURE 6.11 A further example of a scatter graph.

TASK 1

Look at the example line graph presented in Figure 6.9. Complete the following table using words from the list:

had fallen	marginally	drop	slight	compares	represented
revenues	disparity	high	half	plummet	August
downward	fell	spiral	period	between	requires
dropped	upward	peaked	at	by	three times

This graph _____ the sales figures of two divisions within Henderson plc. At the beginning of the year, Division B had _____ the sales of Division A, and this _____ continued throughout the _____. There was an _____ trend in sales from January to _____, after which there was a _____ decline until September, followed by a _____ in sales _____ September and October. During this two-month period, sales _____ from a _____ of £80m to £30m for Division B. Sales for Division A _____ in July _____ £115m, but _____ October they _____ to just under £70m. This _____ a substantial _____ in sales _____ for both divisions. This _____ trend continued until the end of the year when sales for Division A _____ to £5m and just over £40m for Division B, which was _____ better than the January figure of £35m, but in the case of Division A was _____ the January figure of £10m. These figures show cause for concern for the company and the reason for the downward _____ in the second half of the year _____ careful analysis.

TASK 2

Write a short report describing the multiple bar chart in Figure 6.6. Incorporate some of the words and phrases given below in addition to those used in Task 1.

> *rose by x%* (or give a figure rather than a percentage)
> *slight / steady / gradual / dramatic increase / decline / drop*
> *declined to . . . / rose to . . . from . . . in (give the month or year)*
> *fluctuated*
> *reached a peak of / peaked at . . .*

Having read your report, the reader should know:

- the overall trend for each sales method (upward / downward);
- any seasonal fluctuations;
- how each of the sales methods compares from the point of view of sales, volume and seasonal variations;
- which method(s) are the most successful and which, if any, are problematic.

TASK 3

Following are four pie charts showing the number of overweight and obese adults in the UK according to sex. Figures 6.12a and 6.12b show the current situation and Figures 6.13a and 6.13b are the statistics predicted for the next decade. Write a report comparing the current situation with the predicted figures – don't forget to write an introductory sentence explaining what the pie charts are about. Use some of the phrases given below the charts.

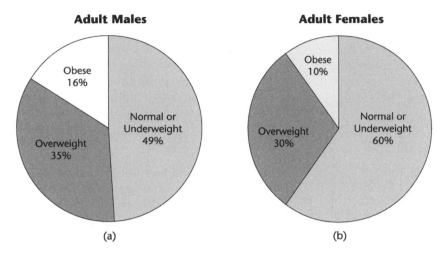

FIGURE 6.12 Pie charts showing the current situation.

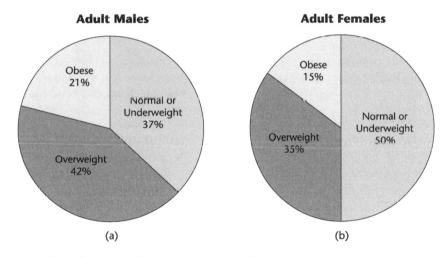

FIGURE 6.13 Pie charts showing the statistics for the next decade.

Here are some useful phrases for predicting trends:

It is predicted that / The prediction is that . . .
This figure will rise to / jump to . . .
Obesity rates are projected to increase by . . .
Compared with males, the rate for females will . . .
The number of adults of normal weight will . . .
If the predicted figures are correct, . . .

TASK KEY

TASK 1

This graph compares the sales figures of two divisions within Henderson plc. At the beginning of the year, Division B had three times the sales of Division A, and this disparity continued throughout the period. There was an upward trend in sales from January to August, after which there was a slight decline until September, followed by a plummet in sales between September and October. From August to October, sales fell from a high of £80m to £30m for Division A. Sales for Division B peaked in July at £115m, but by October they had fallen to just under £70m. This represented a substantial drop in sales revenues for both divisions. This downward trend continued until the end of the year when sales for Division A dropped to £5m and just over £40m for Division B, which was marginally better than the January figure of £35m, but in the case of Division A was half the January figure of £10m. These figures show cause for concern for the company, and the reason for the downward spiral in the second half of the year requires careful analysis.

TASK 2   (Possible answer)

Figure 6.6 presents the sales of Acme Ltd over a twelve-month period. The sales figures shown are broken down into three categories: internet and telephone sales and sales resulting from newspaper and magazine advertisements. Internet sales generally increased over most of the period, except for the last quarter, when they dropped back to around £5,000 in December. This sharp decline was possibly due to technical problems within the company. Internet sales rose gradually from January to May and then shot up in June, reaching a peak of £80,000 in August. September sales remained strong at £70,000 but then declined to less than half that figure during October and November.

Telephone sales were fairly strong throughout the period, starting at £25,000 in January and rising to £45,000 in March. There was a seasonal fluctuation over the summer months, but sales were still steady at £40,000 at the end of the year. Sales made through responses to newspaper and magazine advertisements were also strong, increasing from £18,000 in January to £40,000 at the close of the period.

The highest sales figures overall came during the summer period for all three sales methods, although March was also a good month for telephone sales. All three sales methods are effective, but the Internet would appear to be a better source of sales over the summer months compared to the rest of the year, possibly because in hot weather customers prefer to shop for products on-line rather than purchase from high street retailers. The slump in internet sales in the last quarter requires investigation.

TASK 3 (Possible answer)

Figures 6.12a and 6.12b show how obesity prevalence varies between male and female adults in the UK. Currently, 10% of females are classified as obese compared with 16% of males. Of those adults not classified as obese, a high percentage are overweight – 30% of females and 35% of males, making a total of 40% of females and 51% of males who are above their optimum weight. This has serious health implications for the population as a whole, particularly as some overweight adults may be very near to being obese.

Figures 6.13a and 6.13b show projected data indicating that the percentage of obese and overweight adults will increase further, with 15% of females and 21% of males being classified as obese by the next decade. The figure for overweight females is predicted to rise to 35% compared to 42% for males. As a result, the number of females and males above optimum weight will rise to 50% and 63% respectively. If the predicted figures are correct, more NHS resources will be taken up dealing with weight-related health problems, such as Type 2 diabetes and heart disease. This has serious implications for NHS funding and may require future governments to ration NHS treatment such that only those who are willing to adopt a more healthy diet and lifestyle will receive free care.

6.10 Analysis and discussion

This is the section of your research report where you comment on the results you have obtained from your investigations and assess their significance in light of your objectives, stated hypotheses and the state of the debate in the field as discussed in your literature review. This is a key section because (hopefully) it constitutes the return on careful investment made in a lucid and revealing discussion of the literature earlier on, and in a sound research methodology.

6.10.1 When results do not support your hypotheses

Of course, it is always possible that your results do not support your stated hypotheses; however, although it *may* be a disappointment, this is less a problem than an inconvenience. Provided your results are not a consequence of poor methodology, the fact that they run counter to your hypotheses is itself revealing and need not devalue the research. Indeed, the disconfirmation of hypotheses may often be more interesting and intriguing than confirmation as it raises further important questions that may form the basis of future research, to which you can make reference in your final section on 'Suggestions for Future Research' (see Section 6.11).

When presenting your analysis and discussion, there are three important guidelines to follow, each closely connected to the other two.

6.10.2 Avoid making claims your data cannot support

Be careful not to exaggerate your claims beyond what the data suggests. Making statements that are not justified by the data will make you look naïve and undisciplined and could critically undermine the credibility of your whole study, as well as your credibility as a precise and discriminating researcher. If you do wish to make any questionable claims that are not categorically supported by your data, then it is imperative that you indicate the 'insecure' status of those claims. You can do this by using such expressions as:

> *This might suggest that . . .*
> *It could perhaps be argued that . . .*
> *This could be taken as limited evidence for . . .*
> *One might wish to argue on this basis that . . .*
> *This might be taken as (admittedly scant/frugal) evidence for . . .*
> *Any claims that this might suggest . . . need to be qualified by the fact that . . .*
> *These findings are ambiguous, but might indicate . . .*

6.10.3 Avoid skewing the data to fit your hypotheses: be 'objective'

When interpreting and discussing your results, it is all too easy to read into them evidence in support of your hypotheses, when in reality such evidence may be minimal or even non-existent. Equally, it can be tempting to alter or 'skew' data in order to ensure it corroborates your hypotheses. In other words, researchers tend to see in data what they want to see rather than what is actually there! This is natural and it is therefore crucial to step back, be disciplined, and look at your results objectively. Try to analyse your data from the perspective of somebody else who has no vested interest in the study or its results and is there simply to ensure that interpretations are based strictly on what is evident in the data itself.

6.10.4 Acknowledge the limitations of your study

Very few, if any, research projects are without flaws of some kind or other. Despite the best efforts to construct a well-designed study and to take account of all possible confounding variables, it is almost impossible to cover all bases. This means that the inferences and deductions you are able make may in some cases be less robust than you would ideally wish. What is important is that, where necessary, you clearly acknowledge this fact. All experienced researchers know that there is no such thing as a perfect study, but your readers will want to feel confident that you are insightful and experienced enough to have identified the weaknesses of your study. By recognizing and openly acknowledging any weaknesses, you instil in the reader a greater confidence in all other aspects of your research. Equally, of course, it is important that none of those weaknesses indicate a fundamental flaw in the conception or design of the study.

6.11 Conclusions

Although this section will have much the same form as any other conclusion (see Section 2.2), it will differ in some ways and will typically contain the following three closely connected elements:

- *A discussion of those inferences that can be drawn from your research*: any inferences you make must be supported by the evidence you have provided in previous sections through rational argument and/or the analysis of data.
- *A statement of the contribution your research has made to the field of inquiry*: the key requirement for a thesis is that it adds to the body of knowledge in a particular field by contributing something original. This section is therefore especially important, for in it you will be summarizing the contribution your own research has made, and it is essentially on that basis that it will be judged by the examiners and other scholars who read it.
- *Suggestions for future research*: the most common way to end a dissertation or thesis is to suggest new avenues of investigation based on your own research as documented in your report. In other words, this is where you indicate how future research might build upon your own methods of investigation and the findings they have produced. Part of this may involve highlighting problems that you had with your own approach and, based on your experience, suggesting alternatives to avoid similar such problems recurring.

Remember, no new information should appear in a conclusion, only inferences drawn from information that has already been presented elsewhere in the dissertation/thesis. Avoid unnecessary digressions and do not introduce new arguments.

Keep your concluding statements concise and to the point, present them in a logical order, and make sure they relate back to your research question(s).

 Although there may be a number of concluding paragraphs or sections at different points of a dissertation or thesis, the final conclusion that appears at the end of the work will generally constitute a complete chapter.

6.12 Bibliography

A bibliography is a complete list of references to the works you have consulted during the course of your research. A comprehensive and well laid out bibliography will be an important factor in how positively your work is evaluated by your peers, examiners etc. A good bibliography will

- indicate that you have consulted others' work and are aware of the debate, arguments and practices in your field, particularly as they relate to the subject of your own research;
- add weight and credibility to your statements;
- enable others to check the accuracy of your information and interpretations;
- direct others to works you have found useful and to related publications;
- acknowledge other people's work and ideas (see 'Plagiarism', above);
- enable you and your readers to review the sources of your information;
- show that you are familiar with academic formatting conventions.

6.12.1 How to format your references

It is important to repeat that there are a variety of styles that are used for formatting references. We noted, for example, in Section 2.3 that the Vancouver referencing system – also called the 'author–number' system – is often employed in the science disciplines and uses a number series to indicate references in the body of the text. These references are then listed in the bibliography in the same numerical order as they appear in the body of the text. Look at the following examples:

1. Shepherd G. Neurobiology. Oxford University Press; 1994.
2. Folstein M, Gilman S. Neurobiology of primary dementia. American Psychiatric Press; 1998.
3. Grabe, L. Depression Reassessed. In: P. Davies, S. Mycroft, S. Dixon (eds). New psychological perspectives. Tamley Press; 2007. p. 57–70.
4. Geck MJ, Yoo S, Wang JC. Assessment of cervical ligamentous injury in trauma patients using MRI. J Spinal Disord. 2001; 14(5):371–7.
5. Morse SS. Factors in the emergence of infectious disease. Emerg Infect Dis [serial online] 1995 Jan–Mar [cited 1996 Jue 5]; 1(1):[24 screens]. Available from: URL:http://www.cdc.gov/ncidoc/EID/eid.htm

Be sure to check which style(s) are considered acceptable in your particular field. Once your have opted for a particular style, apply that style consistently and do not jump from one style to another. We shall focus in detail on the Harvard system.

The following examples show how referencing conventions are applied according to their sources:

Books

Personal authors

Clark, A. (2000) *Organisations, competition and the business environment*. London: Pearson.

Brown, G. and Atkins, W. (1990) *Effective teaching*. London: Routledge.

Coffield, F., Borrill, C. and Marshall, S. (1986) *Growing up at the margins: young adults in the North East*. Milton Keynes: Open University Press.

Peters, G. (1990, 2nd edn) *Real-time processing*. London: Routledge.

 Where a book has more than one edition, be sure to state which edition of the book you have used.

Edited volumes

Day, R. editor. (1986) *Talking to learn: conversation in second language acquisition*. Rowley: Newbury House.

Organization as author

British Medical Association. (1993) *Complementary medicine: the BMA guide to good practice*. Oxford: Oxford University Press.

Chapter in a book

Pilfer, M. (1994) 'Quality assurance in higher education', in B. Wilkins (ed.) *Issues in Higher Education*. London: Falmer Press, pp. 77–92.

Major, R. (1987) 'A model for interlanguage phonology', in G. Ioup and S. Weinberger (eds) *Interlanguage Phonology*. Cambridge: Newbury House.

Theses or dissertations

Murray, N. (1996) *Communicative Language Teaching and Language Teacher Education*. Ph.D. thesis. University of London.

Official publications

Department of Health (1998) *1996 Report of the Committees on Toxicity, Mutagenicity, Carcinogenicity of Chemicals in Food, Consumer Products and the Environment*. London: HMSO.

Articles in journals

> Peters, M. (1992) Performance and Accountability in Post-Industrial Society: the crisis of British Universities. *Studies in Higher Education* 17 (2) 123–40.

The first number (17) is the volume number and the second number (2) is the part number (where available). The final numbers (123–40) are the page numbers of the article.

The conventions for joint (two) or multiple (more than two) authorship of articles are the same as those used for books.

Diagrams and illustrations

> Klein F. (2006) Demographic trends in the Indian subcontinent since 1990. in: V. Steppenwolf and M. Khalid (eds) *The Indian Subcontinent: Human Geographical Perspectives*. London: Cyclone Press.

Electronic sources (See also Sections 2.3 and 4.3)

Students are often uncertain how they should cite electronic sources. When citing internet sources, you should include:

- the author's name (if known);
- the full title of the document;
- the www homepage (if available);
- the author's email address (if available);
- the date of publication;
- pathway directions for accessing the document;
- the date you accessed the information.

Example:

Citing in the bibliography:

> Simons, Peter (2001) 'Audience Participation'. Theatre Reviews. *http://www.big brother.terracom/frames_news.html* (15 Oct. 2001)

 Always check your source carefully to see how the title of the article or book was written in the original publication before citing it in the body of your text or the bibliography.

Remember:

- Every publication listed in the bibliography should have been cited in your thesis or used in its preparation.
- Each publication should include the following elements in the order they are presented here:

- author(s) surname(s) plus initial(s);
- date of publication;
- title of book (or title of book in which the work appears if it is a chapter);
- title of journal (if a journal article);
- volume/edition/page numbers (if a journal article);
- place of publication and name of publisher (if a book).

- All sources cited in your thesis should be listed alphabetically in the bibliography by author/organisation.
- If more than one book has been written by the same author (one or more as a single authorship and others in collaboration with other authors) the order in which they should be listed can be seen below. Note that for this order to apply, the single author appearing in category a) must also be the main author (i.e. that listed first) in those subsequent publications appearing in categories b) and c):

a) single-authored items are listed first
b) joint authored items are listed second
c) multiple authored items are listed last.

Within each of these 3 categories (a, b and c) items should be listed in order of date, with the earlier-published items appearing first.

- If two or more items in the bibliography have the same year of publication, they should be listed with a small (lower-case) letter (a, b, c, etc.) following the date. This convention should be followed both within the main body of the work and in the bibliography:

Field, A. (1985a) refers to this as . . .
or (in the Bibliography)
Field, A. (1985a) Issues in Language Teaching. *Education* 165(25) p.560
Field, A. (1985b) Perspectives in the Primary Curriculum. *Cambridge Journal of Education* 15(1) pp.41–9

6.12.2 Bibliographic Management Software

Today there are a number of bibliographic software packages available that make the process of creating a bibliography much easier and less time consuming by automatically generating and formatting reference lists for you. Three such packages are *RefWorks* (www.refworks.com, a Web-based service), *Reference Manager* (see www.refman.com) and *EndNote* (see www.endnote.com). Often, universities will have licensing agreements with the providers of these packages allowing you to download them free to your computer. Alternatively, you can purchase them privately. Bibliographic management software allows you to create a database of references for books, journal articles, book chapters, dissertations, art work, recordings, web pages and so on. These records can be entered manually or imported directly from library catalogues and commercial

databases. The software then uses this database to create and format a bibliography in a specific style while working in word processing software such as
Microsoft Word.

TASK 1

Below is a list of references which have not been formatted. Using the guidelines already outlined, format them correctly, being careful to place them in
alphabetical order and to check your punctuation.

Authors:	John Bender, David Wellbery (editors)
Date:	1990
Title:	The ends of rhetoric: history, theory, practice
Publisher:	Stanford, California: Stanford University Press

Authors:	Dan Sperber, Deirdre Wilson
Date:	1982
Title:	Mutual knowledge and relevance theories of comprehension
Source:	Mutual Knowledge (N. Smith, editor)
Publisher:	London: Academic Press

Author:	Henry G. Widdowson
Date:	1979
Title:	Rules and procedures in discourse analysis
Source:	The development of conversation and discourse (T. Myers, editor)
Publisher:	Edinburgh: Edinburgh University Press

Author:	Howard Felperin
Date:	1985
Title:	Beyond deconstruction
Publisher:	Oxford: Clarendon Press

Author:	Laurence Tribe
Date:	1971
Title:	Trial by mathematics
Publisher:	Harvard Law Review 84: 1329–1393

Author:	Department for Environment, Food and Rural Affairs
Date:	2006
Title:	Animal Health 2006
Publisher:	London, HMSO (Report of Chief Veterinary Officer)

Author:	Henry G. Widdowson
Date:	1979
Title:	Explorations in applied linguistics
Publisher:	Oxford: Oxford University Press

Author: Marga Firle
Date: 1990
Title: The relationship between poetic and verbal communication
Publisher: Poetics: Journal for Empirical Research on Literature, the Media and the Arts. Volume 19, Nos 5–6: 423–431

Author(s): BBC NEWS On-line
Date: November 3, 2006
Title: How we are being watched
Publisher: http://news.bbc.co.uk/2/hi/uk_news/6110866.stm

Authors: G L Nelson, M Al-Batal, E Echols
Date: 1996
Title: Arabic and English compliment responses: potential for pragmatic failure
Publisher: Applied Linguistics 18/3: 411–433

 TASK KEY

TASK 1

BBC NEWS On-line (2006) How we are being watched. http://news.bbc.co.uk/2/hi/uk_news/6110866.stm (3 Nov. 2006).

Bender, J. and Wellbery, D. (eds) (1990) *The ends of rhetoric: history, theory, practice.* Stanford, California: Stanford University Press.

Department for Environment, Food and Rural Affairs (2006) *Animal Health 2006.* London, HMSO (Report of Chief Veterinary Officer).

Felperin, H. (1985) *Beyond deconstruction.* Oxford: Clarendon Press.

Firle, M. 1990 The relationship between poetic and verbal communication. *Poetics: Journal for Empirical Research on Literature, the Media and the Arts.* Volume 19 (5–6): 423–431.

Nelson, G.L. Al-Batal, M. and Echols, E. (1996) Arabic and English compliment responses: potential for pragmatic failure. *Applied Linguistics* 18 (3): 411–433.

Sperber, D. and Wilson, D. 1982 'Mutual knowledge and relevance theories of comprehension', in N. Smith (ed.) *Mutual Knowledge.* London: Academic Press.

Tribe, L. (1971) Trial by mathematics. *Harvard Law Review* 84: 1329–1393.

Widdowson, H.G. (1979a) 'Rules and procedures in discourse analysis', in T. Myers (ed.) *The development of Conversation and Discourse.* Edinburgh: Edinburgh University Press.

Widdowson, H.G. (1979b) *Explorations in applied linguistics.* Oxford: Oxford University Press.

6.13 Appendices

Any material that you feel would interrupt the flow of the main text and act as a distraction from your main arguments, thereby making their comprehension more difficult, should be put into one or more appendices. Material that typically appears in appendices includes lists, questionnaires, documents, tables, glossaries and so on. The reader can then be directed to the appendices at the appropriate point in the dissertation/thesis:

Examples:

See Appendix 3 for a full copy of the questionnaire used.

A copy of the questionnaire used can be found in Appendix 3.

In the circumstances, it was decided that a questionnaire (see Appendix 3) would be the best tool for data collection.

7

. . . And when it's all over: publishing and presenting your research

7.1 Introduction • 7.2 Journal articles • 7.3 A book • 7.4 Conference presentations • 7.5 A final note

7.1 Introduction

All too often, and despite the hard work that has gone into them, completed research reports end up gathering dust in a department cupboard, the university library, or on a bookshelf at home. Once there, the chances are pretty slim that anyone will ever read and therefore benefit from them. This seems a pity at best and irresponsible at worst, but it's the sad reality. Degrees have been awarded partly or wholly on the basis of these reports and the research underpinning them – much of it original and shedding important light on its field. It seems only right, therefore, that it should be brought to the attention of others in the field and the wider academic community, where it may form the basis for new insights and research. There are three main avenues via which this can happen: conference presentations, journal articles and a book. In all three cases an airing of the research helps ensure the researcher's elevation within the profession and promises to get them an additional return on their considerable investment of time and money – and perhaps a title! However, a note of caution: a good research report does not necessarily make a good book, article or series of articles. The requirements of one do not necessarily fit comfortably with the requirements of the other. For example, a highly detailed piece of research which focuses on a minute aspect of a particular area of inquiry, while original and significant, may not appeal to the general readership of a particular journal, and an article presenting it may therefore be rejected on that basis.

7.2 Journal articles

This is probably the most frequently used channel for disseminating research findings. It is common practice to aim to get at least one publication out of your thesis or dissertation. These, if published in a prestigious, highly regarded journal, can significantly enhance your professional standing. In the current research- and publications-led university climate, that can have important implications for your job prospects and career development.

If you do plan to try and publish parts of your research in a journal, there are a few things you'll need to consider. First, each journal will have a particular focus and will only publish research which is in line with that focus. Most journals clearly specify the kind of submissions they are looking for so as to avoid receiving inappropriate material and wasting both journal editors' and authors' time. Those specifications may show a preference not only for articles in a particular field or subject area, but also for empirical or library-based research, for example. You will therefore need to select a journal which offers the most suitable forum for the publication of your article.

The second thing you'll need to consider is the journal's reputation and prestige. While it may be far easier to get your article published in a less prestigious publication, the weight that publication will carry with your professional peers will be proportionately less. Most authors will first target the most respected journals and then work their way down the list if they get no joy. The thinking tends to be that it's better to get a publication in a less highly respected journal that none at all. The most prestigious journals normally have a rigorous peer-review process, where respected figures in the field (normally at least two) will read and comment on the article and make a recommendation for or against publication. This process is usually 'blind' so that the reviewers are unaware of who has written the article. The idea of a blind review process is that it avoids the potential problem of bias in favour of established names in the field and puts everyone on an even playing field. This means that new authors will not be disadvantaged and that, in theory at least, the best quality articles get published regardless of who has written them. There are, however, those who claim that in practice reviewers are sometimes able to recognize particular authors' writing styles or theoretical perspectives!

One of the disadvantages of submitting an article to a more prestigious journal is a reduced likelihood of it being accepted for publication simply because the competition is stronger, particularly from academic heavyweights who may well be more experienced in the publishing game. Furthermore, if it is accepted, the time lapse from original submission to publication will often be longer than in the case of less highly regarded journals – although these too can often have extended publication times. It can take up to six months – sometimes longer – before you receive any response from the editor, and as we'll see later, you may then have to make revisions to the article. Once it is finally ready for publication, it can take up to twelve months for it to appear in print.

Journals are also quite particular about the format of article submissions and will each have their own style guide which will vary between different journals. These guides will advise you on such things as line spacing, margin widths, how to deal with footnotes, the use of titles, headings and sub-headings, how to cite works within the text, and how to format your bibliography. You should check your article carefully before submitting it to ensure that it conforms to these guidelines and does not waste your time and that of the publisher. You should also check how many copies of the article the publisher requires and whether these should be submitted in electronic form and/or hard copy. It is often the case that publishers also request two different versions of the article, one with your name and contact details included, and one without them.

Along with the article you will need to send a short paragraph   usually of around 100–150 words – of biographical data. This is key information that presents a professional profile of who you are, the institution with which you are affiliated, your achievements and interests in the field, and your academic qualifications.

Once your article has been submitted and reviewed there are a number of possible outcomes: first, and most rarely, it may be accepted 'as is' without any changes having to be made. Second, it may be accepted on condition that specified changes are made; third, the journal may feel the article has potential and, on that basis, invite you, the author, to make more substantial changes to it, after which reviewers will have another look at it – but with no guarantee of publication. Finally, it may be rejected. Normally, in all cases, the reviewers' comments will be forwarded to you, usually anonymously. These may then form the basis of any necessary revisions, should you wish to pursue the submission. Should you choose not to do so, the reviewers' feedback will, nevertheless, hopefully serve as a useful guide for any future articles you may choose to submit, and it is in this spirit that it is shared with you.

As with any submission, it's a good idea to look at a few examples of articles successfully published in the journals(s) you are interested in and use these as a model.

Remember, the process of getting an article published can often be a long and difficult one. Be prepared to have your work rejected first time around and to recast it where necessary, but don't lose heart and give up. Do not take rejections personally or interpret them as indicating that your article is not worthy of publication. Remember, the competition is often fierce and what finally gets published can ultimately come down to the decision of one or two individuals. Before submitting an article, consider showing it to an experienced writer who has a record of successfully publishing in journals.

7.3 A book

As with an article, it can take considerable, time, patience and perseverance to get your research published in book form. In addition, it will probably require a good deal of self-belief in the face of criticism, even rejection. Even before your proposal is received, the publisher will already have in place publishing plans based partly on current or anticipated market trends and the extent to which published works are succeeding in responding to those trends. They will therefore consider your proposed book in light of these plans and whether or not it could potentially fill a gap in those plans. It is important to remember, therefore, that rejection is not necessarily a reflection of the quality of your work, but may simply be down to market forces.

7.3.1 The proposal

If you feel your research report has the potential to be turned into a book then the first stage is for you to submit a proposal to a suitable publisher, one who has a tradition of publishing books in your particular field of interest. The idea of a proposal is to give the publisher an idea about the nature of the book and whether it is well conceived, and it will typically consist of the following elements:

• A brief overview or 'synopsis' of the book – its main thrust and the thinking behind writing it.
• A more detailed description of the content, along with a Table of Contents.
• A description of the book's primary (and possibly secondary) market, as you see it, along with an explanation of the competition. This will normally include highlighting specific competitors already out there on the bookshelves and identifying what you regard as their strengths and weaknesses. You will be expected to explain the advantages of the proposed book over each of these competitors, along with its distinguishing features.
• Some sample material – two chapters is fairly common.

- Some other details about the book such as its anticipated length, whether it will include any illustrations – and if so what kind and how many, any ancillary material that is to be included, and any other features.
- A copy of your CV.

Although different publishers may differ slightly in what they ask for and the headings they use, these features are quite standard.

7.3.2 The review process

Once received by the publisher, your proposal will be examined and sent out to reviewers for their comments. The possible outcomes of the review process will be similar to those of article reviews, as described earlier. In the case of a book proposal, if the general feeling of the reviewers is positive, the most likely response from the publisher will be to ask you to rework the proposal responding to the reviewers' and publisher's comments in the process. While you would be expected to give those comments careful consideration, you would not necessarily be expected to agree with them – indeed, it's not unusual for reviewers themselves to express contradictory views; however, if you chose to disagree you would need to provide a rationale for doing so.

7.3.3 Going to contract

The revised proposal will be considered and the publisher will either be satisfied with the new version or request further revisions. Although at any stage they may feel it is not worth investing further time on the project and decline to publish the book, hopefully they will feel reassured by the revisions and, on that basis, offer you a contract the terms and conditions of which will vary according to the publisher, their confidence in the book's market/sales potential, and your experience as an author. In terms of royalties, these tend to be in the range of 8–10%, most likely the former in the case of first-time authors. If you find yourself in the fortunate position of having been offered a contract, it's advisable to show it to a seasoned author in order to ensure that you fully understand its terms and conditions and are not signing up to anything unreasonable or unconventional. Generally, contracts issued by larger publishers are fairly standard and you shouldn't have much to worry about; however, before signing you still need to be fully aware of your and the publisher's commitments under the terms of the contract.

Before a contract is issued, a writing schedule is agreed. Although the publisher will normally aim to get the book to market at a particular time of year when initial sales will be potentially greatest, this is usually negotiable. Once a date for the submission of your manuscript is decided, this will be incorporated into the contract, and you as author will be expected to honour it as far as possible. Although publishers try to be flexible, they usually have clear deadlines to work to; as such there may well be a clause in the contract that gives them the option not to publish if the author fails to meet the deadlines specified in the contract.

7.3.4 The publisher's house style

To help you in your writing and to save time later on, the publisher will provide you with a 'house style'. This is a writing guide that specifies how you should format your manuscript – line spacing, diagrams and so on.

7.4 Conference presentations

Conference presentations are a popular way of getting your research, or parts of it, out there and into the academic community. One of the advantages this channel offers is a greater likelihood of your paper being accepted, although it will still need to meet the approval of a selection committee. While competition can be strong, particularly in the case of high profile international conferences where people hope to enhance their academic reputations and/or air new ideas to a knowledgeable audience, generally you stand a reasonably good chance of having your paper accepted provided it is conceptually sound and potentially of interest to conference attendees, and the proposal is well written. Remember, in the case of key international conferences, paper submissions need to be in well in advance, sometimes as much as nine months, so think well ahead.

Conference presentations can also be a good way of testing your ideas among your professional peers before submitting them to a journal. The feedback you receive may be invaluable. Equally papers that have been submitted to (and hopefully accepted by) journals may well also be good candidates for presentation at conferences.

Finally, post-presentation 'chats' can also be productive not just in terms of the feedback you receive on your ideas but also in that they may lead to invitations to deliver the paper at similar events at tertiary institutions, or to contribute to relevant SIGs (Special Interest Groups).

7.5 A final note

Publishing is never an easy ride, and it can be a painfully slow and frustrating one at times, so be prepared to have to work for that publication! Keep faith with yourself, persevere, and don't lose heart if you fail at your first few attempts.

Part 3

TOOLKIT

8

Punctuation basics: A brief guide to punctuation use

8.1 Introduction • 8.2 Capital letters • 8.3 The comma • 8.4 The semicolon • 8.5 The colon • 8.6 Parentheses • 8.7 Inverted commas (see also Section 2.3) • 8.8 The hyphen • 8.9 The apostrophe

8.1 Introduction

Punctuation marks are an integral part of written English. Among other things, they indicate pauses and sentence boundaries and also help to eliminate ambiguity. A well-punctuated dissertation or thesis should make your work easier to read and understand and will therefore help it make a more favourable impression on your readers. The basic rules of punctuation are, therefore, well worth taking the trouble to learn and apply.

Although entire books have been written on punctuation use, these are often too detailed for practical use, containing as they often do a level of detail that may be admirable in itself and of great interest to a linguist, but which is overwhelming for a student. With this in mind, we have put together a summary of rules governing the most commonly used punctuation marks. Although you will probably be familiar with some of these rules, a number of them, particularly those governing the use of semi-colons and apostrophes, can be a cause of real confusion. Here is our attempt to simplify them for you.

8.2 Capital letters

Most people know that capital letters are used after a full stop (or 'period') to begin a new sentence. However, you may be less familiar with some of the other ways in which capital letters are used in English. They are used

- **for all proper nouns and adjectives and their abbreviated forms**

  England,   English
  the United Kingdom   the UK

- **at the beginning of main words (content words) which form the title of a textbook, journal, play, poem or other publication**

  An Integrated Approach to Business Studies (a textbook title)
  Harvard Business Review (a journal title)

> *Prepositions are not normally capitalized, nor are the words* **a**, **the**, **and**, *unless they are the first letter of the first word of the title. The first word of titles is almost always capitalized and the first letter of content words (i.e. words other than articles or prepositions) of article titles, in particular, are usually all capitalised.*

- **in titles or names used to refer to a specific person or place**

  This was first recorded by Professor Green in experiments conducted at the University of Birmingham.
  The Principal of King's College London had talks with the Secretary of State for Education.

8.3 The comma

The comma is used:

- **to list items** Use commas to separate lists of adjectives and adjectival phrases, nouns and noun phrases, and verbs and verb phrases. For example,

  The course will examine the films of Pasolini, Fellini, de Sica and Zeffirelli.
  (nouns)

He entered the room, sat down, opened his textbook and began to read.
(verb phrases)
The tribe had developed elaborate rituals, complex patterns of social interaction and a very clearly defined social hierarchy.
(adjectival phrases)

In this case commas serve as substitutes for the word 'and'. For this reason, the comma is usually omitted before the last item in a list, where it is replaced by *and*.

- **to separate clauses joined by *and, but, yet, so, for*** These five words are known as coordinating conjunctions and should be used to join two or more sentences. When sentences are combined into one longer sentence using co-ordination, each of the sentences becomes a clause. The comma is placed before each co-ordinating conjunction, *not* after it. For example,

'Captain Corelli's Mandolin' has been a very popular novel, and it has also enjoyed considerable success as a film.

 A comma is not required if the subject of the second clause is the same as that of the first. In this case, the subject does not need to be repeated and the third person singular 'it' can also be dropped.

'Captain Corelli's Mandolin' has been a very popular novel and has also enjoyed considerable success as a film.

- **to separate a word (or group of words) from the sentence it introduces** This use of the comma helps the reader to identify the subject of the sentence and to link it to the previous sentence. In doing so, it helps to make your text cohesive. For example,

Besides volcanoes, earthquakes are another destructive force.

In this example the comma separates the two nouns (*volcanoes* and *earthquakes*) and makes it clear to the reader that the subject of the sentence is 'earthquakes'. 'Besides volcanoes' is merely an introductory phrase that links this fact with a previously mentioned fact about volcanoes.

Words or phrases that link ideas by showing relationships between sentences and paragraphs in this way are known as connectives. They include: *however, nevertheless, therefore, for this reason, consequently, as a result, on the contrary*. For example,

The productivity of agricultural land can be increased by the use of fertilizers; however, natural resources are in finite supply.

It is, nevertheless, regrettable that so many people have had to suffer in order to prove this point.

- **to separate and distinguish subordinate clauses from main clauses** Again, this use of the comma helps the reader to identify the subject of the sentence. The comma is placed at the end of the subordinate clause, immediately before the subject of the main clause. Words which commonly introduce a subordinate clause are *when, because, since (when it means 'because'), as, while, after, before, if, provided that, providing,* and *unless*. For example,

  When the experiment was repeated a week later, the results confirmed previous findings.
  Because some of the conditions specified in the contract had not been met by their suppliers, the company decided to terminate the contract.
  Unless house prices fall over the next twelve months, many first-time buyers will remain priced out of the housing market.
  Provided that all the necessary precautions are taken, the chemical can be used quite safely.

 It is not necessary to use a comma if a sentence begins with the main clause, as in: The chemical can be used quite safely provided that all the necessary precautions are taken.

- **to separate and distinguish inserted information** There are many instances where commas are used to separate words which provide additional, often incidental information, and which are not part of the main sentence. In other words, if this additional information were removed, you would still be left with a perfectly grammatical and meaningful sentence. Although there are many ways of introducing this kind of inserted information, the words *which, who* and *where* are frequently used. For example,

  Arthritis, <u>which attacks the joints</u>, is the single biggest cause of disability in the UK.
  It is, <u>of course</u>, true to say that there are many scholars who disagree with this viewpoint.
  This product has very little future, <u>in my opinion</u>.

 Be careful with these words and other relative pronouns when punctuating; sometimes they are used to limit the subject of the sentence. In this case, they do not take a comma:

The book which was essential reading was entitled 'Principles of Marketing'.

Commas should not be used here because the relative clause *which was essential reading* distinguishes this book from others on the list which were only *recommended* reading. Therefore, the subject 'book' is limited. This type of relative clause is called a 'defining relative clause' because it helps to define and distinguish the subject more precisely. Contrast this with the sentence about arthritis where it is indicated that arthritis attacks the joints in all cases, and in which the subject, arthritis, is therefore not limited. The relative clause in this example is a 'non-defining relative clause' because it does not serve to define or distinguish the subject more precisely.

 The relative pronoun 'that' is not used to introduce a non-defining relative clause.

- **to separate words which explain or describe a preceding noun**

  Monsanto, the American chemical giant, has come in for considerable criticism for its promotion of genetic modification in agriculture.
  The work of Rosalind Franklin, a chemist at King's College London, was crucial to the discovery of the double helix.

8.4 The semicolon

A semicolon functions rather like a bridge or 'halfway house' between a comma and a full stop. It indicates a pause that is longer than that of a comma, but shorter than that of a full stop. Two ideas joined by a semicolon can almost always be written as two separate sentences, and strictly speaking, therefore, semi-colons are not really essential punctuation. Nevertheless, they do serve a very useful purpose by indicating the close relationship that exists between two ideas; a relationship in which the second idea is often an extension or explanation of the first (as in this very sentence you're reading now!).
Use semicolons:

- **when two ideas are closely connected in meaning**

  The monuments of Armenia are more complicated and richer as Arab occupation did not last as long and was less efficacious; the Byzantine influence was also more direct (Lassus 1966).
  Furthermore, consciously or unconsciously, each artist followed what his master had taught him; he was not even free on a technical level (Lassus 1966).

In the damp, mild climate of the UK, farmers can cultivate both spring and winter wheat; they can sow winter wheat from September to February, and spring wheat in March and April.

- when connecting words (*however, therefore, nevertheless*, etc.) are used to join two ideas so closely related that a full stop is unnecessary

Failure is often a difficult thing for managers to cope with; therefore, it is sometimes hidden.
The student's work was not well presented; however, despite this, she achieved a pass.
Raw materials can be quarried, mined or drilled for below the Earth's surface; for example, coal mining, oil drilling and limestone quarrying have been important primary industries in the U.K.

- when recording a list of ideas, each of which is quite long

In the 20th century, people continued to move to urban areas for a variety of reasons; an increasing number of better paid jobs, many of which were cleaner and required more skill than jobs in rural areas; proximity to their place of work; superior housing, services and shopping facilities and more entertainment.

8.5 The colon

The colon is used:

- to introduce an explanation or example(s)

Those wishing to pursue this course have two options open to them: they can take the IELTS examination or the Cambridge Proficiency examination.
Raw materials include everything naturally present in or on the earth prior to processing, and can be collected in three ways:

1. *They can be mined, quarried or drilled for below the earth's surface.*
2. *They can be grown.*
3. *They can be collected from the sea.*

Today, laptop computers are far more suited to the rigours of fieldwork: they are more durable, lighter, and have integrated and highly complex communication and navigation systems, such as GPS.

- to introduce a quotation

  As Schwartz states: 'Peace in Europe has at least as much to do with U.S. involvement in European affairs since 1943 as with France and Germany building the EU'.

8.6 Parentheses

These are also known as brackets. They can be either round ( ) or square [ ]. Round brackets are used:

- to enclose citations within a text

  Capital Bank (http://www.capitalbank.co.uk), which is part of the . . .

- to enclose additional information which is not central to the sentence

  When deciding upon location, retailers consider the impact of micro factors such as pedestrian flows and the nearness of other key retailers in the area (such as Marks & Spencer).

Square brackets are used:

- to enclose words or an idea within a quotation which is not part of the original quotation This use of square brackets is sometimes described as indicating an 'interruption' within a direct quotation. For example,

  As English [sic] shipbuilders and engineers we congratulate our German colleagues on the way their work is being done and the remarkable advances which are being made (Sir William White, quoted in Warren 1966). His reply was typically categorical: 'I appreciate it [the honour], but I must refuse'.

8.7 Inverted commas (see also Section 2.3)

These are also known as quotation marks. There are two kinds of quotation marks, single and double, and although there are no hard and fast rules about when to use double as opposed to single quotation marks, it is important that you are consistent in the way you use both types. The guidance given here reflects the way in which single and double quotation marks are frequently used.

Use single quotation marks:

- **to identify a direct quotation** (see also Section 2.3)

    'Marketing is the management process which identifies, anticipates, and supplies customer requirements efficiently and profitably.' (Chartered Institute of Marketing)

- **to enclose/highlight words which are not accepted as normal English** These may be foreign words with no English equivalent or words used to refer to a new term or concept. For example,

    'Mammismo' is the term used to refer to the close ties the average Italian male has with his mother.
    Some people refer to a 'third Italy' (i.e. an area in addition to the traditional North–South divide)

- **to enclose a word(s) which has a specialised meaning in a particular context**

    'greenfield' site (differs in meaning from the more usual green field*)*
    'Green' companies tend to exploit their environmental awareness when marketing their products.
    Germany is considered to be Europe's largest 'environmental state' with a large number of rigorously-enforced environmental laws.

- **to enclose product names**

    The retailer, Superdrug, asks women to fill in a small questionnaire and then take it to their local store to pick up a 'Mother Pack'.

- **to express doubt over the accuracy or appropriateness of a particular word or phrase**

    The 'view' that we had from the hotel window was of an industrial wasteland.

The word *view* is usually used to describe an attractive outlook or vista, especially within the context of a hotel brochure. By putting the word in single quotation marks, therefore, the suggestion is that an outlook of an industrial wasteland cannot really be appropriately described as a *view*.

Use double quotation marks:

- **to enclose a quotation which is used as part of another quotation**

In discussing the notion of interlanguage, Roberts states:

'The idea of an interlanguage where, in Ellis's words, there exists "a systematic knowledge of a second language which is independent of both the learner's first language and the target language," has dramatically affected the way in which errors are viewed in second language learning' (Ellis 1986).

8.8 The hyphen

The hyphen (-) is used

- **in word units of more than one word (compound words)**

numbers:	twenty-six, eighty-five countries, one-tenth
ranges:	1965-80, 23-5, Manchester-Liverpool, Essex-Suffolk border
	NB: In printed matter these hyphens would be replaced
	by an en dash, and would appear as:
	1965–80, 23–5, Manchester–Liverpool, Essex–Suffolk border
adjectives:	long-wave radiation, north east USA, non-governmental
	organisations, post-industrial experience, less-developed
	areas, high-rise blocks, quasi-natural, life-size, run-down,
	U shaped, new-product development
nouns:	super-organisms, high-technology, psychological well-being,
	microchip-making, land-use, by-product

- **to separate a word which begins on one line and finishes on the following line** You must be careful with this use of the hyphen – try to avoid splitting words at the end of a line. Furthermore, there are certain conventions you must adopt when separating words. In general, words are separated after prefixes (e.g. un-, in-, il-) or before suffixes (e.g. -ment, -ness). Words with double letters are divided between the double letters (at-tachment). The purpose is to create a more natural break and so make it easier for the reader to either predict the complete word or to provide a natural pause. If a word is divided incorrectly, it causes the reader to hesitate and, as a result, slows down the reading process. Here are some examples of good practice.

ir-rigation, govern-ment, ser-vices, unim-peded or un-impeded, hous-ing, ap-pearance, net-works, alterna-tive, Nether-lands.

The hyphen must always be placed after the first part of the word and not on the following line before the second part of the word. Compound words that are hyphenated should be divided across two lines in the same way. Look at the following examples:

| . . . govern-
ment | *not* | . . . govern
-ment | . . . stamp-
collecting | *not* | . . . stamp
-collecting |
| . . . alterna-
tive | *not* | . . . alterna
-tive | . . . bottle-
opener | *not* | . . . bottle
-opener |

Finally, make certain that you put the hyphen above the line and *not* on the line.

- **to signal incidental information**

  Johnson argued - rather courageously given the view of the scientific community at large - that Atlantis amounted to more than simply a product of the imagination of a few romantically inclined pseudo-academics.
  Hoyt's Land-Use model - revolutionary compared to the Burgess model made up of concentric circles - described patterns of land use in cities in terms of sectors.

8.9 The apostrophe

The apostrophe (pronounced 'apostrofee') is one of the most difficult punctuation marks for many students. It is used

- **to show the omission of one or more letters**

  can't (instead of 'cannot'), *isn't* (instead of 'is not'), *it'd* (instead of 'it would')

 Full forms such as cannot, is not *and* it would *are usually preferred in academic writing. Their shortened forms are normally used only in informal writing and, of course, in speech (see Section 3).*

- **to show possession**
  - **a.** where there is a single owner:

    The girl's trousers; Jennifer's trousers; Mary's dog

b. where there is more than one owner:

> *The girls' trousers* (here, there is more than one girl, and therefore probably more than one pair of trousers, although it's possible that they share the same pair of trousers!)
> *The Smiths' house* (a couple with the surname 'Smith' own the property).

In the above two examples, notice the position of the apostrophe.

 If there is more than one owner, but they are mentioned individually, then the last owner mentioned takes the single owner form of the apostrophe. For example,

> *Mr and Mrs Smith's house*
> *Jennifer and Mary's dog*
> *Peter, David and Simon's car*

Some nouns have an irregular plural (child – children; man – men; woman – women); in these cases, the singular and plural owners both take the singular owner form of the apostrophe. For example,

> *child's – children's*
> *man's – men's*
> *woman's – women's*

The two uses of the apostrophe described earlier (showing omission and indicating possession) are often confused by students. As a result, errors such as *it's tail* instead of *its tail* are common in student writing. Remember, only a possessive *noun* takes the apostrophe. Also, be careful to position your apostrophes correctly.

- **to indicate the plural of letters**

> *The word 'accommodation' is spelt with two c's and two m's, while 'recommendations' is spelt with one c and two m's.*

9

Glossary of key terms

Abstract – A written summary that appears at the beginning of your thesis or dissertation.

Acknowledgements – A statement which features at the beginning of your thesis or dissertation and expresses your gratitude to those individuals and/or organizations who have contributed to it in some way.

Anecdotal evidence – Evidence based on personal accounts rather than facts or research and which is therefore not necessarily true or reliable.

Appendices (singular: appendix) – A section or table of supplementary information provided at the end of your dissertation or thesis.

A priori – Something that is assumed without investigation. A type of reasoning or knowledge which proceeds from theoretical deduction rather than from observation or experience.

A posteriori – Reasoning from effects back to their causes. A type of reasoning or knowledge which proceeds from observations or experiences to the deduction of probable causes.

Bibliography – A list of all the books and articles used in the preparation of your thesis or dissertation.

Chronological – Arranged according to date or order of occurrence.

Citation – The act of quoting or mentioning as an example or to support an argument.

Codes of Practice/Rules and Regulations – Usually a booklet, published by a university, which details the administrative and academic procedures governing the writing and submission of a research report.

Coherence – The sense of unity and flow that exists between the ideas expressed in a piece of writing.

Cohesion – The sense of connectedness that exists between sentences and which is created by devices such as linking words and phrases (*therefore, as such, consequently, however* etc.) and pronouns (*him, they, them* etc.).

Concept – A notion or idea

Conclusion – A final statement, usually expressed as a judgement or opinion. A written conclusion will normally draw together the various threads of your foregoing discussion and include new insights based on reasoning from what has been said in the course of that discussion.

Contextualization – The provision of background information as a way of framing and giving meaning and significance to what you say, by putting it into perspective. Context may include what has already been said about a subject, and a statement of where an idea is theoretically located – where it comes from and how and where it 'fits in'.

Data – Facts and statistics collected together for reference or analysis, and used as a basis for inference and reckoning.

Deductive Reasoning – Reasoning based on the inference of particular instances from a general law.

Dissertation – A detailed discourse, especially as submitted for a higher degree in a university.

Empirical Research – Research which is based on observation and experiment. This is in contrast with library-based research, which is purely theoretical.

Ethical Issues – Issues concerning what is morally right and wrong. For example, secretly recording a person's behaviour for research purposes and then including it in your report without first asking their permission is considered unethical behaviour.

Evaluation – To appraise or assess something.

Evidence – A body of facts, objects or reasoning constituting evidence and indicating whether a proposition is true or valid.

Fieldwork – Practical work conducted by a researcher in the natural environment, rather than in a laboratory or office.

Footnotes – An additional piece of (often slightly peripheral but nevertheless relevant) information, numbered and printed at the bottom of a page.

Gender-neutral Language – Language which avoids the use of *he, she, him, her* and *his* in order not to specify the sex of a subject (or subjects) being referred to.

Hypothesis – A supposition or proposed explanation made on the basis of limited evidence as a starting point for further investigation.

Implication – The conclusion that can be drawn from something although it is not explicitly stated.

Inference – A conclusion reached on the basis of evidence and reasoning.

Inductive Reasoning – Reasoning based on the inference of general laws from particular instances.

Introduction – The first main section of a piece of writing in which the writer prepares the reader for the discussion that is to come by placing it in context and giving an indication of the direction it will take.

Library-based Research – Theoretical research which is not based on observation and experiment. Library-based research is normally contrasted with empirical research.

Link Words/Phrases (Transitional Words/Phrases) – Words and phrases which are used to indicate the relationships between different ideas and in so doing create a sense of fluency and coherence.

Literature Review – That section of a research report where the writer gives a summary of work published in the area in order to help frame his/her own research by indicating its relevance to and location within the broader discussion.

Logical argument – A well reasoned argument structure whereby ideas are positioned in relation to each other in such a way that each follows logically from those which precede it.

Methodology – The system of methods used in conducting a research project and which are selected on the basis that they are most likely to achieve the stated goals of that project in the most effective and accurate fashion.

Paragraph – A section of text in which there is one main idea that is developed with the help of supporting information.

Parallel Structure – The structure that results when two or more phrases that mirror each other in terms of their grammatical form are used for the purpose of literary effect; for example, 'These are the voyages of the Starship Enterprise. Her five year mission: *to explore* strange new worlds, *to seek out* new life and new civilizations, *to boldly go* where no man has gone before.'

Paraphrase – To express the meaning of a passage using different wording from the original, often in order to achieve greater clarity.

Plagiarism – The practice of taking someone else's work or ideas and pretending they are your own by not acknowledging their original source.

Premise – A previous statement or proposition from which another is inferred or follows as a conclusion: *if both premises are true, then the conclusion must also be true.*

Primary Source (see also Secondary Source) – A fundamental or original document relating to a particular subject, experiment, time period or event. Autobiographies, scholarly journals, diaries, interviews, field research reports and creative works are examples of primary sources. These sources show authority and thoroughness in discussion of a subject.

Proposal – A formal plan for a research project which is submitted to a university department for consideration. The overall strength of the proposal will be a major factor in the department's decision whether or not to approve your research and/or accept you as a research student.

Qualitative Methodology – An approach to research which involves the collection and analysis of information based on its quality rather than its quantity. It is less concerned with numbers and accurate measurement and more concerned with the depth of data. It will typically involve the collection of that data via Ethnography, Action Research, Participant Observation, Oral History and so on.

Quantitative Methodology – An approach to research in which the data you collect and analyse involves the accurate measurement of phenomena and, often, the application of statistical analysis. It is essentially concerned with numbers and anything that is quantifiable (or measurable) and as such uses methods such as Psychometrics, Statistical Modelling Techniques, Datasets and Services, Experimental Design and Statistical Computing and Methodology.

Quotation – A group of words taken from a text or speech, and repeated *verbatim* in your own writing.

Rationale – A set of reasons or a logical basis for a course of action, idea or belief.

Reference – A source of information cited in a book or article.

Register – The degree of formality in spoken or written language. Research reports are generally written in a more formal register, whereas a letter to a friend will probably be written in a more informal register and may well contain slang and other casual forms of language.

Research – Systematic investigation and study in order to establish facts and reach new conclusions.

Research Etiquette – The rules of appropriate professional behaviour governing the conduct of research.

Research Report – An extended written document – usually a dissertation or a thesis – describing a research project: its motivation, methodology, results and conclusions.

Secondary Source (see also Primary Source) – Materials or sources that are not original but which contain information that has been cited, translated, or based upon another primary or original source. Secondary sources are generally less reliable than primary sources and include textbooks, histories, critiques, commentaries and encyclopaedias.

Sentence Combining – A writing technique that can make writing more efficient, economical and more elegant by expressing in one sentence connected ideas that might otherwise be expressed in two or more sentences.

Spidergram – A graphical technique used for organizing/planning a piece of writing. A spidergram shows the main and supporting ideas in a piece of writing as well as the relationships between ideas.

Subjects – People or animals that are used in a test or experiment.

Summary – A brief statement or account of the main points covered in an entire piece of writing or a particular section of it. A research report may contain a number of summaries in its pages.

Thesis – A long essay involving personal and original research, written by a candidate as the primary requirement for a university degree – usually a PhD.

Thesis Statement – A statement of intent that appears in the introduction to a research report and which makes clear the purpose of the report and what it is you intend to do in the pages that follow.

Title Page – The front page (or cover page) on which is written the title of your research report, along with the role it fulfils as a requirement of your degree, your name, and the date of submission.

Topic Sentence – That sentence in a paragraph (often, the first sentence) which expresses the main idea of that paragraph. The main idea will often be developed through the accompaniment of a number of so-called *supporting sentences*.

Upgrading – The process of formally being transferred from an MPhil-registered student to a PhD- registered student, following a successful internal examination of the progress made in your research project. Many PhD candidates are initially registered as M.Phil. students, and the period prior to the upgrade examination (often an interview) effectively serves as a probationary period.

Validity (of ideas) – A notion that refers to ideas that are soundly based, well-reasoned, supported by strong evidence and logically consistent.

Variable – Something which may vary or change. Variables are those elements, features or factors that impact on your study both negatively and positively, and which you will therefore need to be aware of, designing your methodology accordingly so as to take their influence into account in ensuring that the results of your research are valid.

Writing Functions – Those different categories that explicitly describe the various purposes to which we put our writing. The most common writing functions include: *definition, description, classification, cause–effect, comparison and contrast*, and *argumentation*, and these can be a helpful way to think about the organization of your writing.

10

The academic word list
(Created by Averil Coxhead)

The words listed below are those which, research suggests, appear most frequently in academic writing. Our reasons for including the list are threefold: first, it will allow you the opportunity to raise your awareness of what these words are. As you try to incorporate them into your writing, with time, they should come to mind more easily during the writing process and expand your repertoire of vocabulary and therefore the colour, sophistication and credibility of your writing. Second, with the help of websites such as The Compleat Lexical Tutor (http://www.lextutor.ca), you can look up any of the words on the list (or indeed any other words) and find out how and in what contexts they are most commonly used, via the sample sentences provided. This can be particularly helpful if you are not entirely familiar with the meaning and uses of a word you may have seen quite frequently – it is a well-known fact that students may have a reasonable passive understanding of certain words, but they often lack a good active understanding of them and are not able to employ these words fluently in their own writing. Finally, the very process of engaging in the above activities will help increase your autonomy as a writer. We hope the list is helpful to you.

Note: Numbers indicate the sub-list of the Academic Word List (for example, *abandon* and its family members are in Sub-list 8). Sub-list 1 contains the most frequent words in the list, and Sub-list 10 contains the least frequent.

Abandon	8	Accumulate	8	Adequate	4
Abstract	6	Accurate	6	Adjacent	10
Academy	5	Achieve	2	Adjust	5
Access	4	Acknowledge	6	Administrate	2
Accommodate	9	Acquire	2	Adult	7
Accompany	8	Adapt	7	Advocate	7

Affect	2	Category	2	Conform	8
Aggregate	6	Cease	9	Consent	3
Aid	7	Challenge	5	Consequent	2
Albeit	10	Channel	7	Considerable	3
Allocate	6	Chapter	2	Consist	1
Alter	5	Chart	8	Constant	3
Alternative	3	Chemical	7	Constitute	1
Ambiguous	8	Circumstance	3	Constrain	3
Amend	5	Cite	6	Construct	2
Analogy	9	Civil	4	Consult	5
Analyse	1	Clarify	8	Consume	2
Annual	4	Classic	7	Contact	5
Anticipate	9	Clause	5	Contemporary	8
Apparent	4	Code	4	Context	1
Append	8	Coherent	9	Contract	1
Appreciate	8	Coincide	9	Contradict	8
Approach	1	Collapse	10	Contrary	7
Appropriate	2	Colleague	10	Contrast	4
Approximate	4	Commence	9	Contribute	3
Arbitrary	8	Comment	3	Controversy	9
Area	1	Commission	2	Convene	3
Aspect	2	Commit	4	Converse	9
Assemble	10	Commodity	8	Convert	7
Assess	1	Communicate	4	Convince	10
Assign	6	Community	2	Cooperate	6
Assist	2	Compatible	9	Coordinate	3
Assume	1	Compensate	3	Core	3
Assure	9	Compile	10	Corporate	3
Attach	6	Complement	8	Correspond	3
Attain	9	Complex	2	Couple	7
Attitude	4	Component	3	Create	1
Attribute	4	Compound	5	Credit	2
Author	6	Comprehensive	7	Criteria	3
Authority	1	Comprise	7	Crucial	8
Automate	8	Compute	2	Culture	2
Available	1	Conceive	10	Currency	8
Aware	5	Concentrate	4	Cycle	4
Behalf	9	Concept	1	Data	1
Benefit	1	Conclude	2	Debate	4
Bias	8	Concurrent	9	Decade	7
Bond	6	Conduct	2	Decline	5
Brief	6	Confer	4	Deduce	3
Bulk	9	Confine	9	Define	1
Capable	6	Confirm	7	Definite	7
Capacity	5	Conflict	5	Demonstrate	3

Denote	8	Environment	1	Fund	3
Deny	7	Equate	2	Fundamental	5
Depress	10	Equip	7	Furthermore	6
Derive	1	Equivalent	5	Gender	6
Design	2	Erode	9	Generate	5
Despite	4	Error	4	Generation	5
Detect	8	Establish	1	Globe	7
Deviate	8	Estate	6	Goal	4
Device	9	Estimate	1	Grade	7
Devote	9	Ethic	9	Grant	4
Differentiate	7	Ethnic	4	Guarantee	7
Dimension	4	Evaluate	2	Guideline	8
Diminish	9	Eventual	8	Hence	4
Discrete	5	Evident	1	Hierarchy	7
Discriminate	6	Evolve	5	Highlight	8
Displace	8	Exceed	6	Hypothesis	4
Display	6	Exclude	3	Identical	7
Dispose	7	Exhibit	8	Identify	1
Distinct	2	Expand	5	Ideology	7
Distort	9	Expert	6	Ignorance	6
Distribute	1	Explicit	6	Illustrate	3
Diverse	6	Exploit	8	Image	5
Document	3	Export	1	Immigrate	3
Domain	6	Expose	5	Impact	2
Domestic	4	External	5	Implement	4
Dominate	3	Extract	7	Implicate	4
Draft	5	Facilitate	5	Implicit	8
Drama	8	Factor	1	Imply	3
Duration	9	Feature	2	Impose	4
Dynamic	7	Federal	6	Incentive	6
Economy	1	Fee	6	Incidence	6
Edit	6	File	7	Incline	10
Element	2	Final	2	Income	1
Eliminate	7	Finance	1	Incorporate	6
Emerge	4	Finite	7	Index	6
Emphasis	3	Flexible	6	Indicate	1
Empirical	7	Fluctuate	8	Individual	1
Enable	5	Focus	2	Induce	8
Encounter	10	Format	9	Inevitable	8
Energy	5	Formula	1	Infer	7
Enforce	5	Forthcoming	10	Infrastructure	8
Enhance	6	Foundation	7	Inherent	9
Enormous	10	Found	9	Inhibit	6
Ensure	3	Framework	3	Initial	3
Entity	5	Function	1	Initiate	6

Injure	2	Major	1	Outcome	3
Innovate	7	Manipulate	8	Output	4
Input	6	Manual	9	Overall	4
Insert	7	Margin	5	Overlap	9
Insight	9	Mature	9	Oversees	6
Inspect	8	Maximize	3	Panel	10
Instance	3	Mechanism	4	Paradigm	7
Institute	2	Media	7	Paragraph	8
Instruct	6	Mediate	9	Parallel	4
Integral	9	Medical	5	Parameter	4
Integrate	4	Medium	9	Participate	2
Integrity	10	Mental	5	Partner	3
Intelligence	6	Method	1	Passive	9
Intense	8	Migrate	6	Perceive	2
Interact	3	Military	9	Percent	1
Intermediate	9	Minimal	9	Period	1
Internal	4	Minimise	8	Persist	10
Interpret	1	Minimum	6	Perspective	5
Interval	6	Ministry	6	Phase	4
Intervene	7	Minor	3	Phenomenon	7
Intrinsic	10	Mode	7	Philosophy	3
Invest	2	Modify	5	Physical	3
Investigate	4	Monitor	5	Plus	8
Invoke	10	Motive	6	Policy	1
Involve	1	Mutual	9	Portion	9
Isolate	7	Negate	3	Pose	10
Issue	1	Network	5	Positive	2
Item	2	Neutral	6	Potential	2
Job	4	Nevertheless	6	Practitioner	8
Journal	2	Nonetheless	10	Precede	6
Justify	3	Norm	9	Precise	5
Label	4	Normal	2	Predict	4
Labour	1	Notion	5	Predominant	8
Layer	3	Notwithstanding	10	Preliminary	9
Lecture	6	Nuclear	8	Presume	6
Legal	1	Objective	5	Previous	2
Legislate	1	Obtain	2	Primary	2
Levy	10	Obvious	4	Prime	5
Liberal	5	Occupy	4	Principal	4
License	5	Occur	1	Principle	1
Likewise	10	Odd	10	Prior	4
Link	3	Offset	8	Priority	7
Locate	3	Ongoing	10	Proceed	1
Logic	5	Option	4	Process	1
Maintain	2	Orient	5	Professional	4

Prohibit	7	Reverse	7	Summary	4
Project	4	Revise	8	Supplement	9
Promote	4	Revolution	9	Survey	2
Proportion	3	Rigid	9	Survive	7
Prospect	8	Role	1	Suspend	9
Protocol	9	Route	9	Sustain	5
Psychology	5	Scenario	9	Symbol	5
Publication	7	Schedule	8	Tape	6
Publish	3	Scheme	3	Target	5
Purchase	2	Scope	6	Task	3
Pursue	5	Section	1	Team	9
Qualitative	9	Sector	1	Technical	3
Quote	7	Secure	2	Technique	3
Radical	8	Seek	2	Technology	3
Random	8	Select	2	Temporary	9
Range	2	Sequence	3	Tense	8
Ratio	5	Series	4	Terminate	8
Rational	6	Sex	3	Text	2
React	3	Shift	3	Theme	8
Recover	6	Significant	1	Theory	1
Refine	9	Similar	1	Thereby	8
Regime	4	Simulate	7	Thesis	7
Region	2	So-called	10	Topic	7
Register	3	Sole	7	Trace	6
Regulate	2	Somewhat	7	Tradition	2
Reinforce	8	Source	1	Transfer	2
Reject	5	Specific	1	Transform	6
Relax	9	Specify	3	Transit	5
Release	7	Sphere	9	Transmit	7
Relevant	2	Stable	5	Transport	6
Reluctance	10	Statistics	4	Trend	5
Rely	3	Status	4	Trigger	9
Remove	3	Straightforward	10	Ultimate	7
Require	1	Strategy	2	Undergo	10
Research	1	Stress	4	Underlie	6
Reside	2	Structure	1	Undertake	4
Resolve	4	Style	5	Uniform	8
Resource	2	Submit	7	Unify	9
Respond	1	Subordinate	9	Unique	7
Restore	8	Subsequent	4	Utilise	6
Restrain	9	Subsidy	6	Valid	3
Restrict	2	Substitute	5	Vary	1
Retain	4	Successor	7	Vehicle	8
Reveal	6	Sufficient	3	Version	5
Revenue	5	Sum	4	Via	8

Violate	9	Visual	8	Whereas	5
Virtual	8	Volume	3	Whereby	10
Visible	7	Voluntary	7	Widespread	8
Vision	9	Welfare	5		

Note: Further information on Coxhead's Academic Word List can be accessed via the following link: http://language.massey.ac.nz/staff/awl/index.shtml

11

List of prefixes and suffixes

The following list of prefixes and suffixes may be useful in helping you understand the meaning and formation of English words. Try to learn them. In the right column you might like to add your own examples of words which use the prefixes and suffixes listed in the left column.

Prefixes

PREFIX	MEANING	EXAMPLES
ante-	before	*antedate*
anti-	against, opposite	*antipathy*
auto-	self	*automatic*
bi-	two, twice	*bilingual*
circum-	around	*circumference*
con-, co-, col-, com-	with, together	*conflate*

PREFIX	MEANING	EXAMPLES
counter-	in opposition to	*countermeasure*
de-	down, reversing	*decline*
dis-	negative	*discontinue*
ex-, e-	out, from	*extract*
extra-	outside, beyond	*extraordinary*
hyper-	extremely	*hyperactive*
im-, in-	in, into	*import*
inter-	between, among	*interaction*
macro-	large	*macroeconomics*
mal-	bad, badly	*malady*
micro-	small	*microcosm*
mini-	little, small	*miniscule*
mis-	wrong, unfavourable	*misinterpret*
mono-	one, alone	*monopoly*
multi-	many	*multinational*
non-	no, not	*non-existent*

PREFIX	MEANING	EXAMPLES
pan-	all, worldwide	*pan-European*
post-	behind, after	*postgraduate*
pre-, prim-	first, before	*predict*
pro-	for, before, in favour of	*pro-education*
re-	again, back	*repeating*
semi-	half	*semi-detached*
sub-, sup-	under	*subterranean*
super	larger, stronger	*supervision*
trans-	across	*transcontinental*
tri-	three	*triangulate*
uni-	one, single	*universal*
un-, im-, in-, ir-	no, not, negative	*unstable*
ultra-	beyond, excessive	*ultrasonic*
vice-	deputy	*vice-chairman*

Suffixes

SUFFIX	MEANING	EXAMPLES
-able, ible	capable of being	*predictable*
-ance, -ence	state, condition, quality	*independence*
-ation–tion	condition, the act of	*segregation*
-dom	state, condition, dignity, office	*freedom*
-ee	the object or receiver of action	*addressee*
-er, -ar, -or, -ist	someone who does a particular thing	*geographer*
-ful	full of, characterised by	*harmful*
-ic, -ical	pertaining to	*geographical*
-ious, -ous	having a particular quality, full of,	*mountainous*
-ise, -ize	to give something a particular quality	*modernize*
-ish	like, resembling	*stylish*
-ism	a political or religious belief system	*capitalism*
-ist	someone who has a political or religious belief	*socialist*
-ity	a particular quality	*volcanicity*
-less	without, loose from	*jobless*

PREFIX	MEANING	EXAMPLES
-ly	like, in a particular way	*rapidly*
-ness	state, condition, quality	*steepness*
-ship	condition, skill character, office	*leadership*

12

Appendix

12.1 Citation styles • 12.2 Sample table of contents • 12.3 Sample list of figures • 12.4 Sample list of maps • 12.5 Sample list of photos • 12.6 Sample list of tables

12.1 Citation styles

Humanities

Chicago

- *Writer's Handbook: Chicago Style Documentation*
  http://www.wisc.edu/writing/Handbook/DocChicago.html
- *Quick Reference Guide to the Chicago Style*
  http://www.library.wwu.edu/ref/Refhome/chicago.html
- *Excellent FAQ on Usage in the Chicago Style*
  http://www.press.uchicago.edu/Misc/Chicago/cmosfaq/
- *Online! Guide to Chicago Style*
  http://www.bedfordstmartins.com/online/cite7.html

MLA (Modern Language Association)

- *Writer's Handbook: MLA Style Documentation*
  http://www.wisc.edu/writing/Handbook/DocMLA.html
- *The Documentation Style of the Modern Language Association*
  http://www.newark.ohio-state.edu/~osuwrite/mla.htm
- *MLA Citation Style*
  http://campusgw.library.cornell.edu/newhelp/res_strategy/citing/mla.html

- *Online! Guide to MLA Style*
  http://www.bedfordstmartins.com/online/cite5.html
- *Useful Guide to Parenthetical Documentation*
  http://www.geocities.com/Athens/Acropolis/1623/document.html

Turabian (an academic style that works in other disciplines as well)

- Turabian bibliography samples (Ithaca College Library). Based on the 6th edition of Turabian's *Manual*.
- *Turabian Style: Sample Footnotes and Bibliographic Entries* (6th edition) (Bridgewater State College)
- *Turabian Style Guide* (University of Southern Mississippi Libraries)
- *Turabian Citation Style Examples* (Northwest Missouri State University)

Sciences

ACS (American Chemical Society)

- ACS Style Sheet
  http://www.lehigh.edu/~inhelp/footnote/acs.html
- ACS Books Reference Style Guidelines
  http://pubs.acs.org/books/references.shtml

AMA (American Medical Society)

- AMA Style Guide
  http://healthlinks.washington.edu/hsl/styleguides/ama.html
- AMA Documentation Style
  http://rx.stlcop.edu/wcenter/AMA.htm
- AMA Citation Style
  http://www.liu.edu/cwis/cwp/library/workshop/citama.htm

CBE (Council of Biology Editors)

- *Writer's Handbook: CBE Style Documentation*
  http://www.wisc.edu/writetest/Handbook/DocCBE6.html
- *Online! Guide to CBE Style*
  http://www.bedfordstmartins.com/online/cite8.html
- *CBE Style Form Guide*
  http://www.lib.ohio-state.edu/guides/cbegd.html

IEEE (Institute of Electrical and Electronics Engineers)

- *Handbook: Documentation IEEE Style*
  http://www.ecf.utoronto.ca/~writing/handbook-docum1b.html

- Sample IEEE Documentation Style for References
  http://www.carleton.ca/~nartemev/IEEE_style.html
- Electrical Engineering Citation Style
  http://www.lehigh.edu/~inhelp/footnote/footee.html

NLM (National Library of Medicine)

- *NLM Style Guide*
  http://healthlinks.washington.edu/hsl/styleguides/nlm.html
- *Citing the Internet: A Brief Guide*
  http://nnlm.gov/pnr/news/200107/netcite.html
- National Library of Medicine Recommended Formats for Bibliographic Citation (PDF format)
  http://www.nlm.nih.gov/pubs/formats/internet.pdf

Vancouver (Biological Sciences)

- Introduction to the Vancouver Style
  http://www.lib.monash.edu.au/vl/cite/citeprvr.htm
- Vancouver Style References
  http://www.library.uq.edu.au/training/citation/vancouv.html
- Detailed Explanation of the Vancouver Style
  http://www.acponline.org/journals/annals/01jan97/unifreqr.htm

Social Sciences

AAA (American Anthropological Association)

- Citations and Bibliographic Style for Anthropology Papers
  http://www.usd.edu/anth/handbook/bib.htm
- *AAA Style Handbook* (PDF format)
  http://www.aaanet.org/pubs/style_guide.pdf

APA (American Psychological Association)

- *Writer's Handbook: APA Style Documentation*
  http://www.wisc.edu/writing/Handbook/DocAPA.html
- *APA Style Guide*
  http://www.lib.usm.edu/~instruct/guides/apa.html
- *Bibliography Style Handbook (APA)*
  http://www.english.uiuc.edu/cws/wworkshop/-
  bibliography_style_handbookapa.htm
- APA Style Electronic Format
  http://www.westwords.com/guffey/apa.html
- *Online! Guide to APA Style*
  http://www.bedfordstmartins.com/online/cite6.html

- APA Style.org
  http://www.apastyle.org/elecref.html

APSA (American Political Science Association)

- *Writer's Handbook: APSA Documentation*
  http://www.wisc.edu/writing/Handbook/DocAPSA.html

Legal Style

- Cornell University's Introduction to Basic Legal Citation
  http://www.law.cornell.edu/citation/citation.table.html
- Legal Citation: Using and Understanding Legal Abbreviations
  http://qsilver.queensu.ca/law/legalcit.htm
- Legal Research and Citation Style in the USA
  http://www.rbs0.com/lawcite.htm

Other

- General info on citing web documents
  http://www.lib.berkeley.edu/TeachingLib/Guides/Internet/Style.html
- Recommended Multi-style Links
  http://www.aresearchguide.com/styleguides.html
  http://www.dianahacker.com/resdoc/

Document provided by Turnitin.com and Research Resources. Turnitin allows free distribution and non-profit use of this document in educational settings.

12.2 Sample table of contents

Contents

12.3 Sample list of figures

12.4 Sample list of maps

12.5 Sample list of photos

12.6 Sample list of tables

References

Australian Department of Finance and Administration (2002) *Harvard Style: Style Manual for Authors, Editors and Printers* (6th edn). Sydney: John Wiley & Sons.

Baren, M. (1992) *How It All Began: Stories Behind Those Famous Names*. Skipton: Dalesman.

Booth, P. and Currie, D. (eds) (2003) *The Regulation of Financial Markets*. London: The Institute of Economic Affairs.

Coordination Group Publications Ltd (2003) *GCSE Geography: Complete Revision & Practice*.

Coxhead, A. (2000) *The Academic Word List*. Available at: http://www.vuw.ac.nz/lals/research/awl/index.htm

Cryer, P. (2000) *The Research Student's Guide to Success* (2nd edn). Buckingham: Open University Press.

Davis, W.S. (1986) *Fundamental Computer Concepts*. London: Addison-Wesley.

Dawson, P.A. (1994) *A Handbook for Horticultural Students*. Chichester: RPM Reprographics.

Di Giovanni, J. (2004) Reaching for power. *National Geographic Magazine*, June.

Elcock, W.D. (1960) *The Romance Languages*. London: Faber and Faber.

Ellis, R. (1986) *Understanding Second Language Acquisition*. Oxford. Oxford University Press.

Furlong, A. (1995) *Relevance Theory and Literary Interpretation*. PhD Thesis. University of London.

Gilbert, F. and Clay, D. (1991) *The Norton History of Modern Europe* (4th edn). W.W. Norton & Co.

Greenhill, R. (1971) *British Shipping and Latin America 1840–1930: The Royal Mail Steam Packet Company*. PhD Thesis, University of Exeter.

Griffiths, J.A. (2001) *Modeling the Sensitivity and Response of Shallow Landslide Hydrology to Climate Change and Vegetation in S.E. Spain & S.E. England*. PhD Thesis. King's College London, University of London.

Harvie, C. (1972) *The Age of Revolutions*. Milton Keynes: The Open University.

Henderson, D. (2001) *Anti-liberalism 2000: The Rise of the New Millennium*. London: Institute of Economic Affairs.

Hockman, H. (1998) *Edwardian House Style*. Vicenza: David & Charles.

Hymes, D. (1972) On communicative competence. In J.B. Pride and J. Holmes (eds) *Sociolinguistics*. Harmondsworth: Penguin.

Jansen, H.W. (1995) *History of Art* (5th edn). London: Thames and Hudson.

Keenan, D. (2004) *Smith & Keenan's English Law* (14th edn). London: Pearson Longman.

Lassus, J. (1966) *The Early Christian and Byzantine World*. London: Paul Hamlyn.

Lipsey, R.G. (1975) *Positive Economics* (4th edn). London: Weidenfeld and Nicolson.

Neville, C. (2007) *The Complete Guide to Referencing and Avoiding Plagiarism*. Maidenhead: Open University Press.

O'Mahoney, M. and van Ark, B. (2006) It ain't what you do, it's the way that you do it. *Economic Review* 23(23): pp.

Pearson Education (2001) *A-Level Study Guide: Geography*. Harlow: Pearson Education.

Phillips, E. and Pugh, D. (2000) *How to Get a PhD* (3rd edn). Buckingham: Open University Press.

Popper, K. (1960) *The Poverty of Historicism* (2nd edn). London: Routledge & Kegan Paul.

Ritter, R. (2002) *The Oxford Guide to Style*. Oxford: Oxford University Press.

Thomson, D. (1990) *Europe Since Napoleon*. London: Penguin.

Vass, P.A. (2004) *Plant Diversity and Spacial Discontinuities of the Albany Centre in the South-Eastern Cape, South Africa*. PhD Thesis, King's College London, University of London.

Warren, K. (1998) *Steel, Ships and Men: Cammell Laird, 1824–1993*. Liverpool: Liverpool University Press.

Waugh, D. (1987) *The World*. London: Thomas Nelson.

INDEX

Page numbers for figures have subscript **f**

Related books from Open University Press
Purchase from www.openup.co.uk or order through your local bookseller

DOING YOUR RESEARCH PROJECT
Fourth Edition

Judith Bell

Worldwide bestseller - over 200,000 sold

An invaluable tool for anyone carrying out a research project.

We all learn to do research by actually doing it, but a great deal of time and effort can be wasted and goodwill lost by inadequate preparation. This book provides beginner researchers with the tools to do the job, to help them avoid some of the pitfalls and time-wasting false trails, and to establish good research habits. It takes researchers from the stage of choosing a topic through to the production of a well-planned, methodologically sound, and well-written final report or thesis on time. It is written in plain English and makes no assumptions about previous knowledge.

This new edition of *Doing Your Research Project* includes:

* New chapter on ethics
* Coverage of latest techniques such as grounded theory
* Completely updated coverage of documentary evidence
* Increased examples from health studies
* New referencing, library searching, and literature review chapters

This book is a guide to good practice for beginner researchers in any discipline embarking on undergraduate or postgraduate study, and for professionals in such fields as social science, education, and health.

Contents
*Preface to the fourth edition – Acknowledgements – Introduction – **PART I: Preparing the ground** – Approaches to research – Planning the project – Ethics and integrity in research – Reading, referencing and the management of Information – Libraries and preparing for literature searches – The review of the literature – **PART II: Selecting methods of data collection** – The analysis of documentary evidence (written by Brendan Duffy) – Designing and administering questionnaires – Planning and conducting interviews – Diaries – Observation Studies – **PART III** – Interpreting the evidence and reporting the findings – Writing the report – Postscript – References – Index.*

2005   320pp
Paperback 978–0–335–20660–5
eBook 978–0–335–22418–0

THE COMPLETE GUIDE TO REFERENCING AND AVOIDING PLAGIARISM

Colin Neville

- Why is there so much emphasis on citing sources in some written work?
- How can I be sure I am referencing sources correctly?
- What is plagiarism and how do I avoid it?

There is a great deal of emphasis on accurate referencing in written work for university students, and those writing for professional purposes, but little information on the 'when', the 'why', as well as the 'how' of referencing. This book fills that gap, giving clear guidelines on how to correctly cite from external sources, what constitutes plagiarism, and how it can be avoided.

A unique feature of the book is the comparisons it makes between different referencing styles – such as Harvard, APA, MLA and Numerical referencing styles – which are shown side-by-side. This provides a useful guide for students as they progress through higher education, and particularly for those on combined studies courses – who may be expected to use two, and sometimes three, different referencing styles.

Other special features in the book include:

- Essays demonstrating referencing in action
- Exercises on when to reference, and on what is, and what is not, plagiarism
- A 'Frequently Asked Questions' section on the referencing issues that most often puzzle people
- A detailed guide to referencing electronic sources, and advice on how to choose reliable Internet sites

A Complete Guide to Referencing and Avoiding Plagiarism is essential reading for all students and professionals who need to use referencing to accurately reflect the work of others and avoid plagiarism.

Contents
Preface – Acknowledgements – Referencing – Why reference? – What, when and how to reference – Plagiarism – Referencing styles – Harvard style of referencing – American Psychological Association (APA) and Modern Languages Association (MLA) referencing styles – Numerical referencing styles – Frequently asked questions – Referencing in action: example references – Index.

2007 240pp

ISBN-13: 978 0 335 22089 2   (ISBN-10: 0 335 22089 4) Paperback

ISBN-13: 978 0 335 22090 8   (ISBN-10: 0 335 22090 8) Hardback

GRAMMAR
A FRIENDLY APPROACH

Christine Sinclair

- Do you feel that your writing lets you down?
- Do you have problems turning your thoughts into writing?
- Do you randomly scatter commas throughout your written work and hope for the best?

You are not alone – and this book is just what you need!

This is a grammar book with a difference. It brings grammar to life by giving examples of grammatical problems in the contexts where they arise by including a soap opera. As the characters' grammar improves, so will yours.

It blends a story about three students – Barbara, Kim and Abel – with advice on specific areas of grammar. The characters' story builds throughout the book, but each chapter can be read separately if readers want to focus on specific grammatical issues.

The book examines and clearly explains aspects of grammar, language use and punctuation such as:

- Academic language
- Standard English
- Correct use of tenses
- Active and passive voices
- Sentence construction and punctuation
- When and where to place an apostrophe
- Using grammar checkers

There are exercises to encourage the reader to relate the issues to their own practice and experiences, as well as an extensive glossary which defines the terms that are used throughout the book.

Grammar: A Friendly Approach is based around issues at university but students from schools and colleges will also love this irreverent look at the rules of grammar: Their teachers and tutors will also see rapid and noticeable improvements in students' written work.

Contents
Introduction – Bad language – Mangling and dangling participles – Getting tense with verbs – Active and passive voices – What is the subject? – The complete sentence – Relationships and relatives – How to be offensive with punctuation – Possessive apostrophes and missing letters – Checking the checker – Finale – Glossary – Appendices – Bibliography – Index.

March 2007   144pp

978–0–335–22008–3 (Paperback)   978–0–335–22009–0 (Hardback)